# Flowers for Embroidery

RICHARD BOX'S

*Flowers*

*for*

*Embroidery*

a step-by-step approach

# RICHARD BOX

*Photography by Dudley Moss*

B. T. Batsford Ltd • London

*For my amanuensis*

A catalogue record for this book is available from the British Library.

ISBN 0 7134 8667 8

Printed in Spain
for the publishers B.T. Batsford Ltd.,
9 Blenheim Court, Brewery Road,
London N7 9NT

A member of the Chrysalis Group plc

**Plate 1 Frontispiece**
'GERANIUMS'. FABRIC COLLAGE,
MACHINE AND HAND
EMBROIDERY, 1986

**Plate 2 Below**
REGENCY WAISTCOAT (DETAIL)
C1800.
LONG AND SHORT STITCHES
WITH FLOSS SILK ON SILK
TAFFETA.
(*HALL-TOWNLEY COLLECTION*)

# CONTENTS

# INTRODUCTION

*Flowers are the beautiful hieroglyphics of Nature*
*by which she indicates how much she loves us.*

GOETHE

Flowers are universally acknowledged to be the most lovely and graceful creatures which Nature produces. Because of their beauty we use flowers at the most important moments in our lives, employing them like ambassadors to communicate all kinds of messages, feelings and emotions. Above all, flowers communicate our love for each other:

*Love's language may be talked with these to work*
*out choicest sentences.*

ELIZABETH BARRETT BROWNING

If we were to look at the entire history of embroidery we should find that flowers are one of the most popular of subjects to be used as decorative motifs. This book is for those of you who continue to follow in this tradition, and it may not surprise you to learn that I also am its follower. I have been drawing, painting and embroidering flowers for many years. I am delighted to have this opportunity to use them now to fashion and form this book for you.

It is my intention to develop some of the ideas, procedures, methods and techniques which I intro-

(LEFT) *Plate 3*
CANVASWORK FIRESCREEN (DETAIL), 1992.
DESIGNED AND WORKED BY PAULINE FARRAR. THE COMPOSITION CONSISTS OF A NUMBER OF FLOWERS REPRESENTING ALL THE SEASONS OF THE YEAR.
THIS DETAIL IS OF THE SPRING-FLOWERING FRITILLARIA.
NOTICE HOW THE SMALL, BUT ALL-IMPORTANT, INCLUSION OF TINY RED STITCHES ENLIVENS THE NEUTRAL COLOURS OF THE FLOWERS AND ENRICHES THE SHADOWS OF THE SURROUNDING LEAVES.

duced in my first book *Drawing and Design for Embroidery—A Course for the Fearful* (Batsford). Although it would help if you had read this earlier book, I hasten to assure you that it is not absolutely necessary.

Whether you are an extremely accomplished embroiderer or a terrified beginner, I shall treat you as if we had only just met. Furthermore, we shall *all* consider ourselves as beginners, because whatever age we are, whatever stage of ability and level of understanding, we are always at the start of some new development, standing at the threshold of new and emerging delights and wonders, all of which are just asking us to explore and discover them.

> *The understanding which we want is an insistent present. The only use of knowledge of the past is to equip us for the present. The present contains all that there is, it is holy ground, for it is the past and it is the future.*
>
> A.N.WHITEHEAD

In order to ease your development and to help further your ability in designing and creating embroideries, I ask you to treat this book as if it were an adventure, a 'voyage of discovery'. All the chapters are composed of projects for you to try; the first three explain everything in detail, the remaining four are devised to give you the chance to practise similar procedures, methods and techniques with different subjects and in different ways. Each stage leads you to the next, so avoid missing any of them and jumping about the book. Rather, use it as if it were a developmental course, whose pages will gradually unfold with new possibilities. Learning can sometimes be a frightening and even a threatening experience. So follow each project in sequence so that the learning experience is one of delight and wonder for you.

One of this book's most important features is that we shall be engaged in more than one project in each chapter, and that we shall explore and investigate them concurrently. Rather than desperately trying to finish one embroidery before we 'allow' ourselves to start another, we shall leave our first attempt at a certain stage so we can shift our attention to beginning another project, and return-

A CONTEMPLATION UPON FLOWERS

*Brave flowers—that I could gallant it like you,*
*And be as little vain!*
*You come abroad, and make a harmless show,*
*And to your beds of earth again.*
*You are not proud: you know your birth:*
*For your embroider'd garments are from earth.*

*You do obey your months and times, but I*
*Would have it ever Spring:*
*My fate would know no Winter, never die,*
*Nor think of such a thing.*
*O that I could my bed of earth but view*
*And smile, and look as cheerfully as you!*

HENRY KING,
*BISHOP OF CHICHESTER*

ing to the earlier project a little later on. This procedure has a number of advantages:

We all know that if we engage in an activity for too long we become tired, not only physically with aches and pains, but also muddled in mind and feeling debilitated in spirit. And yet, how often do we give ourselves a rest immediately? If we are honest, we say 'I'll just do this little bit first'; and half-an-hour later we find ourselves still engaged in the same activity, without having made any progress and altogether more irritable! On reflection we need to admit that to leave a problem for a while and to return to it later often yields the solution with unexpected speed. Hence, why not start another project?

Furthermore, if we allow ourselves a number of different ways of approaching a similar problem, it gives us a psychological advantage. It allows a more adventurous spirit to flourish and we can afford to take risks because there would be the safety of other projects in reserve.

Having a number of concurrent projects also facilitates the transference of ideas: it encourages a freedom of spirit, a flexibility of mind and a fluency of skill so that new discoveries will greet us in rapid succession. With similar speed we can transfer their revelations from one project to another. Such discoveries may be quite simple, but they are nevertheless important; such as how comfortably we are sitting in the chair, how we set out our equipment, or in what ways we might cut the material. At other times they might be more complex; such as a dramatic colour combination, or a dynamic movement created by a particular direction of a series of lines, or a subtle balance of contrasting textures. Each new discovery is as important in its own particular way as another, and each one needs cherishing, nurturing and consolidating. This can be done most effectively by regular practice, and it must be accomplished quickly because if it is left for too long there is a risk that it will all be forgotten.

However, let us not dwell any longer on the theory alone, but immediately put these ideas into practice.

# $\mathcal{P}$OPPIES

We are slumberous poppies,
Lords of Lethe downs,
Some awake and some asleep,
Sleeping in our crowns.
What perchance our dreams may know,
Let our serious beauty show.

Central depth of purple,
Leaves more bright than rose,
Who shall tell what brightest thought
Out of darkest grows?
Who, through what funeral pain
Souls to love and peace attain?

Visions aye are on us,
Unto eyes of power,
Pluto's always setting sun,
And Proserpine's bower:
There, like bees, the pale souls come
For our drink with drowsy hum.

Taste, ye mortals, also;
Milky-hearted, we;
Taste, but with a reverent care;
Active-patient be.
Too much gladness brings to gloom
Those who on the gods presume.

LEIGH HUNT

*Plate 4*
'Poppies and Daisies'.
Fabric collage, machine and
hand embroidery, 1989

The poppy is the subject for our first project because it is a flower which delights so many people. It certainly gives me great joy, so imagine my pleasure when I found a whole field of them and for several days was able to devote my attention to exploring their strange character. Their fragile strength has always seemed a paradox: their colour is as vibrant as the sound of trumpets, whereas their form is as thin and frail as nearly transparent tissue; their heads rise with pride to greet the sunshine, but by late afternoon seem so full of its warmth that they are compelled to bow down, subsiding into sleep. Indeed, poppies have always been associated with sleep and consolation. According to legend, the goddess Ceres, mourning for her lost daughter Proserpine, created the poppy so that she could eat its seeds and forget her grief.

> *Indulgent Ceres knew its worth,*
> *When to adorn the teeming earth,*
> *She bade the poppy rise;*
> *Not merely gay, the sight to please,*
> *But blest with power, mankind to ease,*
> *And close the aching eyes.*

HORACE SMITH

These scarlet splendours make a spectacular subject for our first study in fabric collage and machine and hand embroidery.

## The Selection

As this is our first project, the design is intentionally kept simple and uncomplicated. It is a very small section taken from one of my paintings (PLATE 5). A helpful way of selecting part from a large area is to make two right-angled 'corners' in the form of a capital letter L, and to choose your section using these like a viewfinder; this not only helps you find the section which pleases you most, but also helps define the particular proportion and shape of rectangle you want.

You may like to follow my design for this project, or you may prefer to use another picture (and this applies to the designs for all the other projects in this book). Perhaps you have a photograph which you took yourself, or you may have another source like a magazine cutting, postcards or your own coloured drawings and paintings. Whatever you choose, keep it clear and simple by selecting an area with obviously contrasting colours and tones. Notice that in mine there are only four blooms, and a clear distinction between red and green and between pale and dark tones.

## The Pattern

Cut a sheet of tracing paper so it is exactly the same size and shape as the rectangle chosen from the original picture with the viewfinder. Place it over the chosen section of the picture, and with a pencil trace all the main contours; the pattern should look like a jig-saw puzzle for a five-year-old! The result should show you what each part of the pattern represents. Compare my pattern in Fig 1 with the section of the original picture. Notice the definite distinction between the red and the green areas, and also the difference between the paler and the darker reds. Always remember that the pattern is for our own use, therefore we do not need to complicate things unnecessarily.

Within the green area it seemed important to indicate the direction of some of the curving lines which represent the stems and buds, because this would help with the directing and placing of the fabric and threads. For reasons of simplicity I did not include all the lines, and I removed those that represented the daisies. I decided to alter the position of the lines and slightly changed their directions, the reason for this is that all the lines were curving in one way only, and I wanted some to go in the opposite direction in order to balance the harmony of my composition.

As this book gradually proceeds, I shall show you many ways to achieve a harmonious balance in designing and creating our embroideries. A recurring theme which we shall explore and develop is: the repetition of similarities, and the contrast of differences.

The repetition of similar elements helps to hold and bind the composition together; it is for this reason that in the poppy design, for example, I

***Fig 1***
PATTERN FOR THE POPPY
PROJECT

preserved many of the curving lines repeating themselves in the same direction. The contrast of different elements helps to give the composition its shape and form: it is how it is seen, and imbues its life with interest and vitality. This is why I changed the direction of some of these curving lines. Too much repetition could lead to predictability, tedium, even banality; too much contrast could result in awkwardness, unrest and even chaos. A proper balance and a sensible combination of repetition and contrast

together create the total harmony and unity of the design and the completeness and integrity of the composition.

The actual size of my pattern is already A5, that is, approximately 150mm (6in) high and 210mm (8in) wide. This is quite an appropriate size for our first project: neither too large, which might take a long time to do, nor too small which can be finicky. There are some occasions, especially when a section has been taken from a small photograph, when the pattern needs enlarging. The easiest way to do this is to have it enlarged at your nearest photocopying establishment, and it is extremely helpful to have several copies made. We shall be using at least two copies here, maybe three.

## *Selecting the Fabrics*

Choose some kind of firm fabric for the background support. Hessian is very suitable because it is strong enough to be stitched by the sewing machine without using a hoop or a frame. It is also loosely woven, so that when it is time for hand embroidery, the needle can be pushed quite easily through both it and the applied fabric. In size it needs to be 115–150mm (4–6in) larger than the paper pattern so that you have a margin of 50–75mm (2–3in) for turning when stretching.

The colour of the hessian you choose should be an important colour in the picture; green covers the largest area in mine, so that is the colour I have chosen to use. However, do not worry if you cannot find hessian in anything other than its naturally light-brown colour. In this project it can all be covered at the early, fabric collage stage. Otherwise you can dye the hessian beforehand, or simply use another kind of fabric which is green; though remember, it is essential that you select a firm fabric.

Finally, at this stage, it is as well to find a way to prevent the edges fraying because trailing threads can be a nuisance. I have sewn my edges in a matching green thread with a wide zigzag stitch on the sewing machine.

We now need to choose the fabrics for the start of this project, which is the collage stage. Some people prefer to use the term 'appliqué', and this is quite appropriate when fabric is applied to fabric. However, as we shall be using an adhesive at this stage, it is actually more accurate to describe the process as 'collage', since this term derives from the French *coller* meaning 'to stick'.

Rummage now in your rag-bag. Indeed, spill its contents out all over the floor! Dive into it with relish and start to put particular groups of colours in

***Plate 5***
'POPPY FIELD'.
OIL PAINTING, 1991

separate piles. Choose about ten or twelve different reds to begin with, in a wide variety ranging from reds that could be classed almost as orange, those that are verging on violet like magenta, and that colour often known as shocking pink. Choose also a wide variety from dark to mid-toned reds and from mid-toned to very pale reds, often called pinks. There is no need for a vast amount of any of these fabrics; the merest scrap, no more than 50mm (2in) will be more than sufficient. However, do not be afraid to use as many *kinds* of fabric as you can: you can use almost anything ranging from velvets to Crimplene. However, I suggest you avoid carpets as the sewing machine does not respond to them very well. I speak from the experience of my over-enthusiastic past!

It is great fun to select fabrics that are quite different from each other. Try to contrast the rough with the smooth, the shiny with the matt and the sumptuous with the ordinary; you will see that, as in this project, each fabric will be cut in small pieces and distributed throughout the picture, where appropriate, once again putting into practice the balance between repetition and contrast in order to create harmony in our design.

The same kind of variety can be applied when selecting the green fabric. Choose some greens that are biased towards blue, such as those that resemble the gem-stone turquoise; and some that are biased towards yellow, like the colour of limes or unripe lemons. Furthermore, some of your fabrics may be patterned and have more than one colour contained therein. This is all to your advantage!

Some of my fabrics are patterned. One of my red pieces has the colour violet as part of its woven design, and several of my greens have yellow and blue as part of their pattern. Yellow and blue are the components of green, and the employment of these two colours in a green area often produces a scintillating effect. So also do metallic elements. Many of my fabrics have glittering passages, and if you desire such an effect it is important when selecting a fabric to determine the colour of the glittering element. For example the colour of silver is white, copper is red and gold is yellow. When this is understood it is easier to know where they can be used.

Finally at this stage all the fabric pieces might be ironed, though this is not absolutely necessary; for instance you might decide not to iron all of them because sometimes the odd wrinkle can add a particular quality to the design. Furthermore, do not be concerned if some of your edges begin to fray, because the contrast between a frayed and a clean-cut edge can be an important contribution to the design.

## The Fabric Collage

It is most important to undertake any project feeling relaxed, and with the right equipment at hand. Thus you will need:

1 A restful mind and a happy heart
2 A clear working surface
3 A comfortable, but upright chair
4 The fabric scraps set out in small individual piles of various reds and greens
5 Two pairs of scissors, one for paper and the other for fabric
6 The backing fabric, such as hessian
7 The paper pattern, see Fig 1
8 A small brush
9 A pot of PVA adhesive, like Marvin Medium
10 The source material, ie PLATE 5: the oil painting of the Poppyfield

First of all ensure that you are sitting comfortably and that you are in a relaxed, but alert, state of mind and heart. If we approach our project in a state of peaceful and quiet attention, our task is more likely to proceed smoothly and efficiently, and most important of all, it will be much more enjoyable to do.

It is not possible to remove problems and difficulties. In fact they are important for creative growth. However, it *is* possible to learn how to approach them with a sense of serious fun and a proper spirit of adventure. So, if you know of some simple relaxing exercises to help you to become calm, then please practise them; do everything you can to ensure the first of our requirements, namely the restful mind and happy heart.

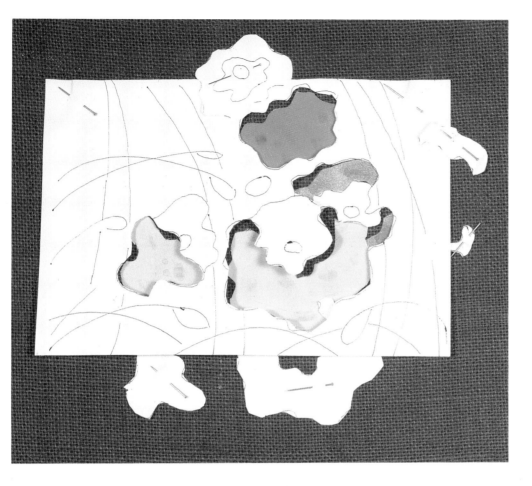

**Plate 6**
START WITH PALE REDS

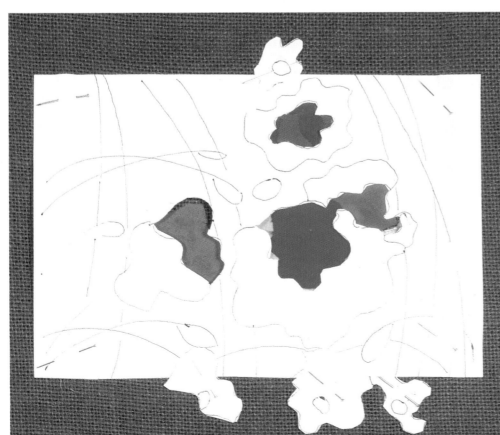

**Plate 7**
USE ANOTHER COPY OF THE
SAME PATTERN FOR DARK REDS

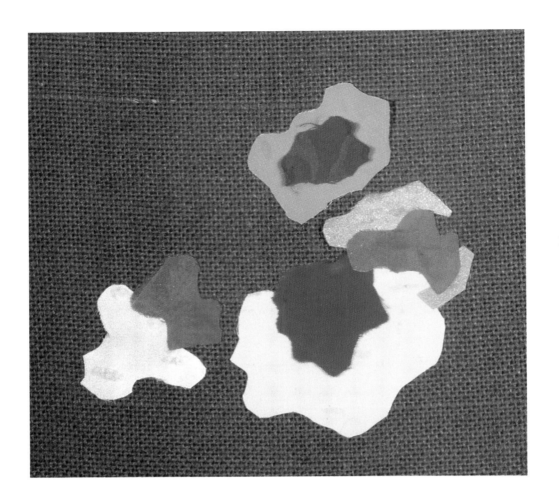

*Plate 8*
INSPECT THE BALANCE BETWEEN
THE PALE AND DARK REDS

*Plate 9*
COMPLETION OF RED AREAS

It is helpful to clear the surface of the worktable so that the start is fresh and clean. As with the mind and heart, if physical practice is chaotic, the same kind of disorder prevails in the work. Being orderly helps us to release ourselves from impediments and lead us towards and along the path to creative freedom.

Lay out all your fabric pieces in different coloured piles all around the edge of the table. Place the green hessian fabric in the centre of the table, but also near to you so that you can reach it easily. Position one copy of your paper pattern on the hessian and put the other copies to one side for later on. You will need a pair of paper scissors and another pair for cutting the fabric; try not to get them muddled, because cutting paper blunts the blades. Finally you will need a brush and a small pot of adhesive. The brush can be quite small and inexpensive; it should have only a few hairs or bristles, but they should form a point at the end so that only a very small amount of adhesive can be taken up. A PVA adhesive like Marvin Medium by Berol will be very suitable because it dries transparently and is easy to sew through when it is dry; a well stocked art shop should have a supply. It is helpful to dispense some into a smaller container such as a miniature jam jar with a screw-top lid.

Attend now to the piles of your fabric pieces: to start with, choose a colour which plays an important role in the picture. You will see in PLATE 6 that I have chosen the pale reds. Cut out all those areas which require that particular colour, and also the particular *tone* of that colour, from the paper pattern. Pin these pieces to those pale-red fabrics of your choice so that you may use them as templates. You can pin them to match either the weave or the bias of the fabric. Technically it does not matter which way, because later on we shall be doing so much sewing over the fabric that any puckering that might occur can be modified. Besides, any such puckering can contribute an attractive variation in texture.

Once more, it is important to put into practice repetition and contrast. Try to use each piece of fabric more than once in the picture, and also try to use it in different ways. In my example (PLATE 6) I have actually used only two different fabrics. The repetition is in the use of the same two fabrics more than once. The contrast is between one matt and one shiny fabric. Moreover, by reversing each fabric there is another, albeit slight, difference in the range from shiny to matt.

This last example of repetition and contrast might be considered so slight as to be insignificant. Sometimes, however, small things are crucial, like lynch-pins and keystones. Often they go unnoticed or their subtlety is considered simplistic, but such simple things are all-important. Our embroideries must have a firm structure, since no amount of cosmetic disguising can hide fundamental faults. Just as houses which are built on sand will crumble and collapse, whereas those on rock remain safe and sound.

Compare this way of working with organic growth. My intention throughout all the projects in this book (as in all my work) is that they should be 'complete' at every stage: a tiny sapling is not a full-grown tree, but it is nonetheless complete even at its early stage of growth. Similarly, a tiny baby is no adult, but is still a completely whole and integrated being. When the baby grows, all parts grow together and each part is related to all other parts, and so on to adulthood.

It is not irrelevant to develop this analogy a little further at this early stage. Many years ago I received a letter from someone whose advice I still find immensely valuable. The passage from that letter was rather more concerned with human beings than embroidery, but nevertheless can you see the connection?

*No good really leaving one or two areas of ourselves behind and growing in the rest. The neglected ones will at some point come into the foreground and be very noticeable and painful. Then the only thing to do is to accept that they are 'younger' than the rest of us and need to 'be brought up to the level of the rest', as someone put it.*

SISTER COLUMBA OSB

Bearing this in mind, let us put such precepts into practice. If you place the remaining part of the paper pattern on to the green hessian backing fabric you will observe the holes which have occurred by your earlier cutting and removal of the paper used as templates. These holes now show you where to

This may seem like a contradiction of that intention to leave the picture complete at every stage: in fact it is an elaboration of that point. Although each stage should seem complete and integrated, it is also right sometimes to accept certain elements as rather clumsy and slightly unresolved. Sometimes in a musical composition, a phrase on its own may sound discordant; and in truth it *is* discordant! Only when this phrase is heard in the context of the whole opus can its contribution be properly comprehended as a necessary part of the entirety of the composition. Similarly, although errors and mistakes are very painful at the time, even *they* can be considered helpful elements in the creative learning process when a wider view is taken. The noble sentiments in the following passage acted as a guide for many years of my life as an embroiderer and painter:

*The parts being so connected that if any of them be either transposed or taken away, the whole will be destroyed or changed; for if the presence or absence of something make no difference it is not part of the whole.*

ARISTOTLE

Let us now continue with our collage and bear these sentiments in mind. Attend to the pile of mid- to dark-toned reds and choose some that you would like to use. Take up another copy of the paper pattern and cut away the four areas which represent this colour in PLATE 7. Here the fabric on the extreme left and right is the same. The piece at the very top is a brocaded fabric, and the one below it is velvet, a different fabric but of a similar tone. Thus even at this early stage I am content with the balance of colours and tones.

I can now remove the paper pattern (PLATE 8) and inspect the pale reds in conjunction with the dark reds, and also their relationship with the green background. Obviously no single element can be seen in isolation, as it is always next to something: nevertheless it is important to emphasise this fact because colours and tones can appear different when their context is altered. My assessment of the picture so far is that although it is crude, the colours and tones seem balanced and 'complete' at this stage. So what is needed now is refinement: smaller

place the pale-red fabric and are thus acting as a stencil. Cut out each pale-red area from the fabric, and as you do so, place each piece in its appropriate position on to the backing fabric. Once you are content with the balance of these pale-red pieces at this very 'young' but 'complete' stage of the project, fix each piece with tiny specks of the adhesive, using only enough to keep the fabric in position. If some of your fabric is very thin you may find that the adhesive shows through. This is nothing to worry about because when the adhesive dries, it merely darkens the fabric slightly, and yields rather an interesting effect as if the fabric itself were slightly mottled. Even if the darkening effect is not appropriate, it is possible to hide such a defect by either laying thicker fabric on top, or waiting till the next stage when subsequent stitching by machine or by hand may gently include and integrate what is now seen as an unsightly blemish.

pieces need including, a greater range of colours and tones need to be added, and more variation in texture would be an advantage.

PLATE 9 shows the completion of the next stage. I found that it was not necessary to use the pattern because both the pale-red and the mid-toned red areas were placed in large pieces and this was enough to guide the positioning of the smaller pieces on top. A certain amount of overlapping is quite acceptable, though try not to have too many layers because subsequent stitching, particularly hand embroidery, may become hard work. Three or four layers should not cause any problems. It was absolutely essential that I looked closely at the original painting to help me determine what kind of shapes, their sizes, and what kind of curved or straight edges to cut. I had to select more fabric, and also to repeat some which was used before in order to preserve the rhythm of repetition and contrast so that a continued balance was always maintained. You will see it is only at this stage that the illusion of poppies begins to emerge.

Turn now to your pile of green fabric and take up another copy of the paper pattern. The reason for using several copies is that some cuts would have to go through previous cuts, particularly at this stage, and it saves time if you do not have to stick all the pieces of the pattern back together. Cut the pattern into three or four pieces along some of those lines which represent the swaying stems. These curves, if you use the pattern like a stencil, will help you to direct and place the green fabric (PLATE 10 shows the completion of this stage). An explanation of the procedure is given here, and you can follow it or find a variation within the scheme.

As before, it was essential that I kept referring back to the painting: the variety and range of fabric has already been mentioned, and once again, the cutting was very important and varied. Some edges are curved, others are straight; some pieces have three sides, others have four and even five. Thus as many differences as were possible were achieved, even to the extent of sticking down yarns to create the illusion of stems and to provide a contrast between narrow and broad passages. Every attempt was made to keep the balance between the extremes of repetition and contrast. For technical reasons it is

always important that the composition should seem balanced and in harmony with itself. It is much easier to rip pieces off at this stage than when they are all sewn down. For artistic reasons you will find that the next stages will go much more smoothly if you have everything in terms of shape, tone, colour and texture in more or less the right place *now*. Embroidery is concerned with embellishment. Although corrections and alterations can be made with stitchery, my advice is to try and make any corrections at this stage. Ensure that the foundations are firm so that your embroidery will have a safe and secure structure to build on, with sumptuous embellishment and ornament.

### Interlude

In the introduction I suggested that it is helpful to be involved in a number of projects concurrently, and here already is an opportunity for us to put this into practice. Often in a project we come to a point of over-involvement and cannot decide how to continue. So, start another fabric collage and take it to the same 'complete' stage as your first one while you still have all your materials and collage equipment at hand. To prevent the change being too sudden, continue with the same subject.

Look at PLATES 15, 16 and 17 which demonstrate slight variations in composition and approach. If you are feeling very adventurous, you could also try another *two* variations on the same theme, even try working these two concurrently. For example when you have just finished using a particular colour in one picture, take that colour immediately through the other picture so that they can both grow and develop together. However, they can be encouraged to develop individual characters: thus although you may use the same colour in each picture, you do not have to use the same materials. Try using one group of materials in one picture and a different selection in the other. Or you could try a variation of tonal range between the two pictures: perhaps one could be much paler than the other. You could even make a very slight but subtle difference in effect by the way you cut the material using the same materials for each picture, cut the pieces very small for

*Plate 10*
COMPLETION OF THE COLLAGE
STAGE

one, and a moderate size for the other. There will be many ideas that will occur to you. Try them all! After all, the very enjoyment of doing these projects lies in experimentation. You will find you work surprisingly quickly, also that the usual worries concerning the end result are diminished and because you are attending to the process rather than the final results, many splendid embroideries arise as a rewarding consequence.

*Proper attention to the finishing, strengthening of the means, is what we need. With the means all right, the end must come.*

SWAMI VIVEKANANDA

Before you go on to the next stage take a look at your first collage to see if there is anything you would like to alter, change or modify as a result of discovering something new in the course of the exercise just described.

## Machine Embroidery

For this stage you will need the following:
1 Your fabric collage
2 A range of red and green machine sewing and embroidery threads. Madeira Threads present a vast, varied and exciting range which are also very reliable. Also try other makes such as Sylko, DMC, Anchor and even those from your local market: all will offer various and different qualities and effects.
3 A sewing machine that will either 'drop' its 'feed' or has a plate which will cover it. It should also have a darning foot. These two devices enable you to embroider freely without having to resort to a hoop or frame, so long as the background fabric is firm, like hessian. For many years I have been devoted to a Bernina sewing machine, though recently I have been introduced to a Pfaff. Both have different but equally excellent qualities.

*Plate 11*
SEW SPARINGLY AT THIS STAGE

Choose a coloured thread to start with. Perhaps it would be a wise plan to follow the same sequence as we did for the fabric collage: so let us start with the pale red. It is as well to have the same colour underneath on your bobbin or spool. Many people advise not to worry unduly about this and to have any colour underneath; indeed so did I once, until I noticed tiny specks of the underneath thread appearing above, and that its colour was quite inappropriate. One follows all the instructions in the sewing machine guide book about tension adjustments, yet even the experts do not achieve exactitude all the time. Nevertheless, such mistakes can sometimes produce interesting effects and can then, as we have said, be employed on purpose. However, we are still only on our first project, and I must not alarm you with too many alternatives. So, wind onto your bobbin or spool the same colour as you use on the top, and keep to this rule throughout all the projects in this book.

Now clip on your darning foot, and ensure that you have a fairly thick needle; its size round about 90 or 100 will effect a prominent puncture through all the layers we have accumulated. Set the stitch-width knob or button to the widest zigzag: curiously enough the wider the stitch, the less it is noticed; the narrower the stitch, such as a straight stitch, the more obvious is its direction. This stage is not so much concerned with statement as with understatement. Our composition and arrangements of directions and movements have been clearly stated at the fabric collage stage; now is the time to soften and moderate such statements. If emphasis is required it can be put in later on, with hand-stitching and, even later, with more machine-stitching. Remember that what is omitted is, perhaps, more important than what is included.

Next, drop or cover the feed. Set the stitch-length to a 'still' position; it is important to spare its unnecessary wear and tear on your machine. Set its tension according to the instructions in the hand-book so that it sews freely and easily over the material with your feed dropped (or covered) and the darning foot attached. It would help to practise on a spare piece of hessian to test that it is sewing smoothly and that you feel comfortable with this arrangement.

Now sew over and across all those pieces of fabric which match the colour and tone of this thread, namely, the pale-red areas. In order to integrate and unify the composition further still, it helps to take this thread into all other parts of the picture where appropriate. The following guide showing you where to go, and how much of it to use in particular areas, should help you in all the projects in this book; it is a guide which has become almost a golden rule for me throughout recent years. Here it is:

For ninety per cent of the area within the picture put each coloured thread onto fabric which is of the same *colour* and *tone*. In this instance the pale-red thread needs to be stitched onto the pale-red fabric. For five per cent of the area it is possible to put these threads on *any other coloured* fabric so long as it is the *same tone*. In this instance the pale-red threads can be stitched onto the pale-green and the yellow fabric, and also onto the reflective and glittering areas because in light, these appear as a *pale tone*.

For the last five per cent any thread can be made to travel across any fabric of any colour and any tone; however, please remember it is only five per cent! Yet curiously enough it is this last five per cent which really invigorates the composition; it is like the hot spice in a dish of chili con carne, which is crucial, but of all the ingredients the smallest in quantity. Once again we can see that this is another manifestation of how the contrast of differences can give life to our compositions when employed in conjunction with the binding force of repeating similarities. Both are important: neither can exist without the other.

Follow this practice with each tone of each colour throughout the picture. Vary the pale reds, the mid-toned to dark reds and also the greens. PLATE 11 shows how important it is to sew very sparingly at this stage: for a picture which is this small size, each

particular thread travels for quite a short time. At this stage the example shown has just two pale-red threads, one mid-toned red thread and two green threads stitched on to it; moreover each piece of fabric has only a few stitches through it. Try to avoid over-developing particular parts of the picture and leaving the rest behind; it is all-important to allow the composition to develop as a whole. If you feel you are getting over-involved you can always take a rest from this project and resume one or more of your other related ones.

PLATE 12 shows the next stage, and how many more threads can be taken throughout the whole composition. As well as variations of the colours which have already been used, small quantities of blue and yellow threads are used to match and link with the vestiges of those colours, the components of green, evident in the green fabric. Notice how the mid-toned red thread is allowed to travel throughout the green areas but in very small quantities. Likewise you can see that a tiny amount of dark-green thread is present in some of the red fabric of the same tone.

## Hand Embroidery

The machine embroidery stage can help to soften hard and abrupt edges, can modulate a rather sudden difference between colour and tone, and can change what might have been crude or even brash at the collage stage to a state with more subtle and graceful qualities. Nevertheless it is possible to do too much stitching and thereby flatten the surface. I have been disappointed sometimes by the loss of the textural differences and contrasts which were present at the completion of the collage stage. However, a remedy is available! Hand-stitching can restore the variety and richness of textural qualities.

Choose a variety of threads. Try using knitting and weaving yarns as well as traditional embroidery wools, cottons and silks. PLATE 13 shows all these, and also some other curiosities, including for example some thick Raffene (which was all the rage in 1960 when our lampshades were covered with it). It has a wonderful glossy sheen, and makes a rather loud but pleasing sound when it is pulled through the fabric. But beware! I have discovered that my

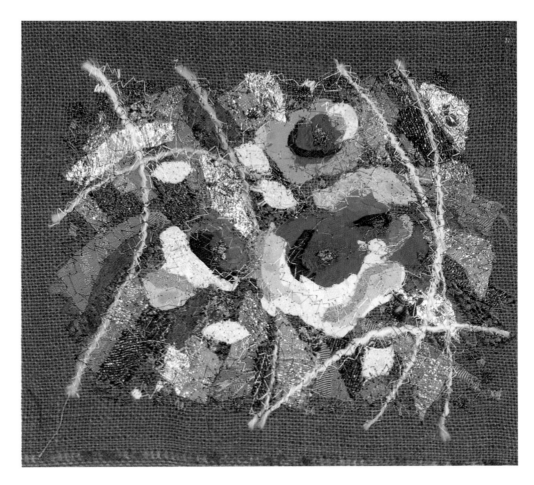

*Plate 12*
MORE THREADS HAVE BEEN
TAKEN THROUGH THE WHOLE
COMPOSITION

*Plate 13*
TRY USING KNITTING AND
WEAVING YARNS AS WELL AS
TRADITIONAL EMBROIDERY
THREADS

*Plate 14*
COMPLETION OF THE POPPY
PROJECT, 1991

cats also find it 'pleasing'. Other threads in this example are variegated, and this helps in depicting the ever-changing quality of light on stems swaying in the sunshine: some are glittering and shiny, others are dull and matt, some are thick and clumpy, others are thin and fine. Once again a deliberate choice was made to juggle with similar and contrasting elements.

Only straight (or stroke) stitch has been used in this example, as it can be worked in any direction and of any desired length. Within its simplicity I have tried to push the possible variations to their limits. Some stitches are long, others are short, and the variety of the threads themselves yields the width of the stitch. Their direction is multifarious and is chosen for three main reasons: firstly, to depict the more natural, lifelike features of the elements in the picture, such as the wrinkles in the petals of the poppies and the line of the stems. Secondly, the direction helps both to emphasise and to refine the rhythm and movement within the design. Finally, the various directions are positioned so as to maintain a balanced harmony throughout the composition.

Remember that you can return to any of your other related projects at any time you like. Try also to leave them 'complete' at any stage, before turning your attention to another.

## Conclusion

Somehow or other the hand-stitching in this project seemed slightly separate from the rest; in fact this was because it was resting on top of all the other elements in the picture. The hand-stitching was rather too pronounced, too sudden in relief and creating an unresolved aspect in the design. PLATE 14 shows the final stage of this project. In order to integrate the hand-stitching with all the other elements, I found it necessary to take the work back to the sewing machine, and with a straight stitch this time I sewed over the hand-stitching. This couching technique seemed to bring all the elements of the design together and to effect a balanced harmony throughout the composition.

I hope *you* are pleased with what you have discovered at each stage in this project, and that you are happy and content to continue.

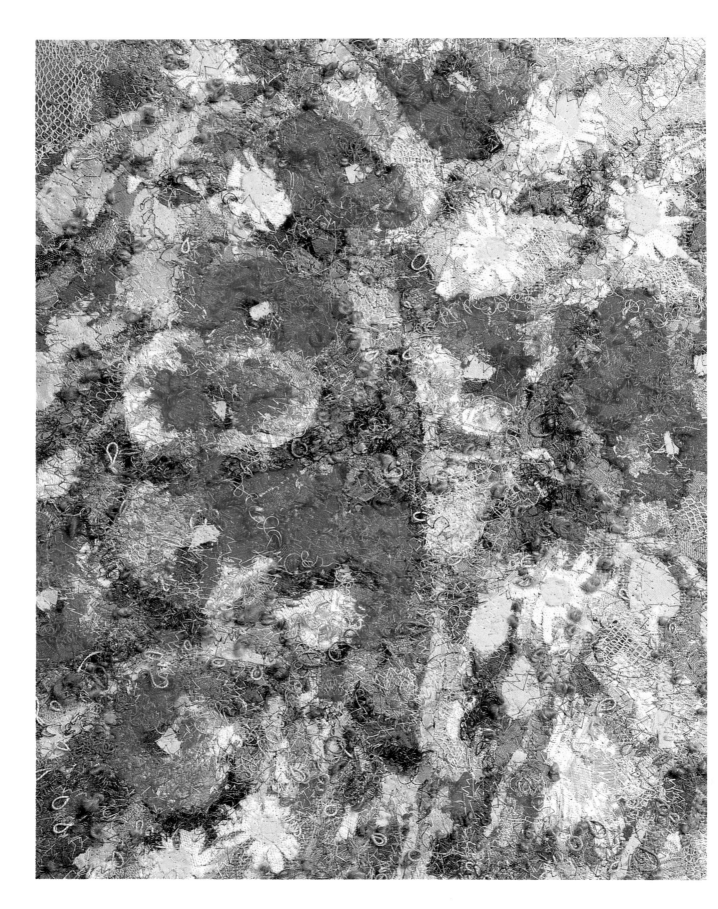

*Plates 15–17*
THREE VARIATIONS ON THE
POPPY PROJECT

Richard Box · July 1991

# $\mathscr{P}$LUMBAGO

FROM: ENDYMION

*A thing of beauty is a joy for ever:*
*Its loveliness increases; it will never*
*Pass into nothingness; but still will keep*
*A bower quiet for us, and a sleep*
*Full of sweet dreams, and health, and quiet*
*breathing.*
*Therefore, on every morrow, are we wreathing*
*A flowery band to bind us to the earth,*
*Spite of despondence.*

JOHN KEATS

*Plate 18*
'PLUMBAGO'. OIL PAINTING,
1991

This chapter is planned for you to practise and consolidate those methods tried with the poppies in the previous project. The flower subject is different and there are slight variations in the technique and in interpretation, but the approach and overall procedure is exactly as before, so there is nothing here that should alarm you; on the contrary, everything is here to encourage you and give you confidence.

In Somerset there is a grand mansion which was once the home of Lord North. To one side of the building is attached a large Victorian conservatory, and in late July and early August one can behold there a magnificent spectacle. Against one of its walls, fashioned from the warm, honey-coloured local stone, grows a spreading plant with flowers that form themselves in clusters and are of an exquisitely delicate pale blue. Its name is 'plumbago'.

The house is Dillington. It became a residential college for adult education, and for many years I have been fortunate enough to teach there in summer. Early every morning, armed with brushes, canvas and oil paints, I would treat myself to half-an-hour's devotion to this lovely creature. I have chosen one of my more recent studies, which particularly emphasises the contrast of the flowers with the pale-orange wall, to serve as impetus and guide for our next project.

You might like to follow my design for this (PLATE 18), or you may prefer to use another picture of plumbago. The choice is yours. We shall be following the same procedure as before, that is by starting with fabric collage and then progressing to machine- and hand-stitching. Nevertheless, there will be a few variations in the way we interpret the method, and later on, there will be a slight change in some of the stitchery.

### The Selection

The size of the oil painting of plumbago is about 460 × 360mm (18 × 14in). Compared with the earlier painting of poppies it is actually quite small. Furthermore, whereas the painting of the poppies was a large view of the field from which we chose a very small part as our design, the painting of plumbago is a small detail of a very large plant; because of this the whole of the picture is used as the design for this project, and it is kept to this size. Therefore this second project will be substantially larger than the first one.

### The Pattern

There are five main areas in this design: the first two are the areas of light and shade on the wall; the next three are those depicting the leaves, the flowers and the thin delicate lines denoting the stalks and stems. As with our first project it is important to put in only the main contours; remember that the pattern is for our own use, and if too many details were included at this early stage it might lead to confusion. However, this design *is* complicated, and exemplifies how it really *is* necessary to have several copies of the pattern available. Figs 2, 3, 4 and 5 overleaf show how by emphasising those areas, *and only those areas*, when we deal with them at each stage, it will

help the procedure to progress more easily.

Deliberate asymmetry is present in this design. However, in order to maintain a balanced harmony in its composition, there needs to be a regular play of repeated and contrasted elements. For instance there are more leaves and flowers to the left of the picture, although there are a few to the right; subsequently there is more of the wall present to the right of the picture, although small areas of it are allowed to appear between the leaves and flowers on the left. If this were not so, the left side of the composition would seem rather too solid, dense and heavy.

Except for the four straight sides of the picture, every edge and contour within the picture itself is curved. This linking repetition is contrasted by the evident differences among the tones and the obvious changes in the colours. These we shall explore more fully when we come to selecting and applying the fabrics at the collage stage.

### Selecting the Fabrics

Some people may only have a limited supply of coloured hessian, so I have used a colour which is not prominent in the picture, just to demonstrate that it is possible to use any colour because the collage pieces can completely cover any background fabric. Obviously it is preferable to use a colour that *does* play some part in the picture so that a little of the background fabric can be allowed to show through where the same coloured collage pieces are applied; this also makes hand-stitching easier in these areas because the collage is not so dense. The coloured hessian used for the last project has been used for this one, too. Follow the same instructions for preparing the fabric. Cut it slightly larger than the size of the intended picture so as to leave a margin of about 50 to 75mm (2 to 3in); remember to sew around the edges to prevent the material from fraying.

The colour of the wall is actually a pale brown. However, when painting it, I found that pale yellows and pale oranges were needed in order to realise its warm honey-coloured effect when illuminated by the sunshine. The illusion of shadows on the wall

*Fig 2*
PATTERN FOR THE PLUMBAGO
PROJECT, EMPHASISING THE
WALL

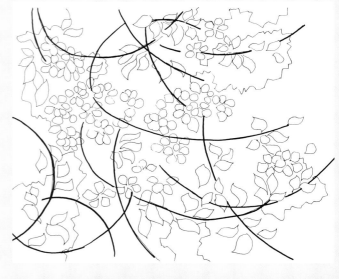

*Fig 3*
PATTERN FOR THE PLUMBAGO
PROJECT, EMPHASISING THE
STEMS

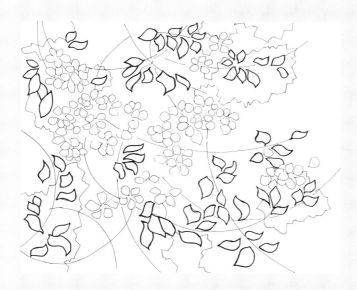

*Fig 4*
PATTERN FOR THE PLUMBAGO
PROJECT, EMPHASISING THE
LEAVES

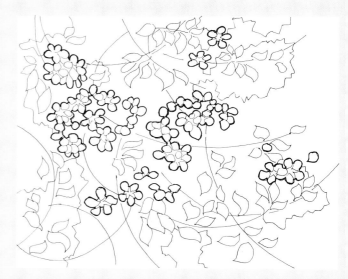

*Fig 5*
PATTERN FOR THE PLUMBAGO
PROJECT, EMPHASISING THE
FLOWERS

was achieved by mixing other colours very thinly and applying them over the yellow and orange painted areas when they were dry. This method is called glazing. The most effective colours were violet and blue, because in thin transparent layers over yellows and oranges they created unexpected and rather subtle greys and cool browns.

*'Art is a lie that makes us realise the truth.'*

PABLO PICASSO

In painting and embroidery we can convey with colour our visual response to these wonderful flowers in their splendid surroundings. At this stage we need to be courageous! Therefore out of your rag-bag seek pale yellows and pale oranges, as well as pale browns such as beiges and fawns to represent the sunlit areas of the wall. Then select pale violets and purples as well as greys for the areas of the wall in shadow. Choose many greens, ranging from very pale to very dark and those ranging from a blue-green to a yellow-green. However, be slightly more cautious with the blues; stay with the kind of blue which is rather more biased towards purple than green, that colour commonly known as royal blue and sometimes as ultramarine. Nevertheless, continue to choose a wide range of tones in that category of blue, so that you have some of a mid-tone progressing to some so pale that they seem almost as white as snow.

As you are selecting the different colours and tones of your fabrics, choose as many different kinds as well. Try to find a range of various textures, just as for the poppy project, because it is this kind of variety which invigorates the life of the picture.

### Problems With Colour

Many of us have difficulties with colour; however try to remember these three points:

Firstly, all colours belong to each other and can harmonise with each other. Physical scientists have discovered that they are all components of white light, and if they come from the same source they are all part of the same family. If we need any more proof we have only to look at the enormous variety of colour combinations in the world of flowers to see how all colours harmonise with each other.

Secondly, remember the distinction between colour and tone, and that although colour and tone are distinguishable qualities, they are inseparable in nature. *Colour* refers to the differences between those qualities which we understand as red, orange, yellow and so forth; *tone* (or 'tonal value', or even 'value') refers to how any one particular colour can range from pale to dark. Sometimes a pale tone is referred to as a 'tint', and a dark tone is referred to as a 'shade'.

This leads to the third point: 'hue' is a term which often refers to that quality which distinguishes one particular type of one colour from another type within the same category. For example, the hue of blue required for the flowers for this project could be described as royal blue or ultramarine, as distinct from the greenish hue of blue commonly called turquoise. In future the word 'hue' will be used in this sense only.

### The Fabric Collage

It is important to start your project in a suitable frame of mind and with the right sort of equipment. You will therefore need:

1 A happy heart and tranquil mind
2 A working surface clear of clutter
3 A comfortable, upright chair
4 The fabric scraps set out in small individual piles:
   *a) pale oranges, yellows and browns (beiges and fawns);*
   *b) pale violets, purples and greys;*
   *c) a range of tones and hues of green from pale to dark and from yellow-green to blue-green;*
   *d) a range of tones of blue from pale to dark but whose hue is within only the purple-blue range, such as ultramarine and royal blues.*
5 Two pairs of scissors, one for paper and the other for fabric
6 The hessian backing fabric
7 The paper pattern
8 A small brush
9 A pot of PVA adhesive

*Plate 19*
COMPLETION OF THE FIRST PART
OF THE COLLAGE STAGE

*Plate 20*
COMPLETION OF THE WHOLE OF
THE COLLAGE STAGE

10 The source material in this case the oil painting of plumbago (PLATE 18)

First of all, ensure that you are comfortable and that you have all the necessary equipment organised and laid out efficiently, just as we did for the first project. Although the subject and the selection of fabric are different, the procedure at this stage is exactly the same as before.

In the project with poppies we constructed the shapes of the flowers first; this was because the flower heads themselves were quite large and took up a substantial area within the design as a whole. Also the contour of the poppy, being a single-headed flower, is relatively simple compared with the multi-headed complexity of the plumbago cluster. Therefore because of this difference we shall begin this project by representing the areas of the wall first, and in particular the shadowed areas.

Cut from one of the copies of your paper pattern (Fig 2) those parts which represent the shadowed areas, and place the rest of the pattern onto the hessian background. This will act as a stencil (the cutaway pieces will not be used as templates as in the poppy project, so you can throw them away). The picture is much bigger than before, and because the area of the wall is so large we can proceed in a more generalised, rather than a specific manner. Cut the pale grey, violet and purple fabric into small fragments; vary their sizes and shapes slightly, and place them near at hand in individual piles. Using the stencil to guide you, assemble these pieces in appropriate places and secure them with very small amounts of adhesive. Your assemblage may very well take on the effect of a floppy mosaic, and this is exactly as it should be! It is always possible to overlap slightly some of the edges of the fabric scraps. When all the shadowed areas of the wall have been constructed, remove the paper pattern (the stencil) and cover the rest of the hessian with small pieces of pale yellow, orange and brown fabric.

Check to see whether there are any sudden changes in tone at this stage in your collage. There needs to be only a slight distinction so far. I have found it helpful to place a few very small pieces of pale yellow and pale orange on top of the pale violet

and grey, and vice versa, so that more subtle changes of tone and also of colour can be realised. If you have transparent fabrics such as nets, gauzes and organdies in these colours, it is an excellent opportunity to use them at this stage. You will be making the equivalent of the glazing techniques in the painting, mentioned earlier.

*When the contrast between light and shade is too violent, a picture lacks beauty.*

LEONARDO DA VINCI

PLATE 19 shows the completion of this early stage. On top of the collage pieces representing the wall in light and shade, you will see that yarns have been applied in curves. These represent the lines of the stalks and stems. In order to convey the changing play of light I have used a variegated weaving yarn. If you cut into another copy of the paper pattern along the lines which represent the stalks and stems (Fig 3), you can use the edges left by the cut paper as a guide to help you secure the yarns in their correct position. Although it is important to make every attempt to achieve a sense of completeness at each stage of these projects, do not worry unduly if certain parts seem slightly clumsy or crude; remember, this is often a necessary part of development.

PLATE 20 shows the next and final stage of the fabric collage. You will find it helpful to have two more copies of the paper pattern (Figs 4 and 5), one for the leaves and one for the flower clusters. From the first, cut all those areas which represent the green leaves; I found it necessary to cut all the leaves individually, even when they appeared in masses. When an area is large, it is possible to generalise, but when the area diminishes in size, as with these leaves, it is necessary to be specific. I have discovered that at this stage it is important to make certain of clear edges and contours in the cutting. If any understating and suffusion is needed, it is easier to do this later. Likewise it is much more difficult to clarify and emphasise details from something made amorphous or even ill-proportioned early on.

All the petals of the plumbago flowers were cut individually as well. Try to start by deploying the darkest blues from your tonal range first and slowly develop to your palest; in this way you will see the

illusion of light gradually giving form to the flowers. To enhance this illumination I have included small pieces of white fabric as the lightest parts of the petals of the flowers.

## Using Colour Constructively

We have already started to use colour in a way that is more than merely 'descriptive', meaning simply that the flowers are blue, the leaves are green and the wall pale brown. Thus in order to portray the play of dappled light on the wall we have used pale yellows and pale oranges as well as beiges and browns. To represent a rich glow in shadowed areas we have employed pale purples and violets together with greys. This is more than a descriptive use of colour. By exaggeration we are using it as a visual metaphor to express our response to the natural world.

**Exactitude is not the truth.**

HENRI MATISSE

Let us push this point further: if we want to enhance any colour in order to make it more noticeable, prominent and powerful, we can do so in two different ways. First, we can place it against a different tone. This is why I exaggerated the paleness of the lightest parts of the flowers by including white. Furthermore, if you look at PLATE 20 you will see I made sure that these white areas were mostly set against dark areas.

The second way to enhance a colour is to place it next to its complementary colour. Glance back to the poppy project and you will notice how prominently the red flowers appear. This is because they are juxtaposed with red's complementary colour, green. And if you look again at PLATE 19 which shows the completion of the first stage of the collage of this plumbago project, you will see that the shadowed areas, even though they may be rough and crude at

*Plate 21*
'PLUMBAGO'. FABRIC COLLAGE,
MACHINE AND HAND
EMBROIDERY, 1988

this stage, have a quality of vitality about them. This is because violet is the complementary colour to yellow, which we used in the sunlit areas. Now look again at PLATE 20 which shows the final stage of the collage, and you will see that the blueness of the flowers is enhanced because they are placed against occasional passages of orange, blue's complementary colour.

This is what I mean by using colour constructively. It is also another manifestation of that important element of *contrast*, which invigorates the life of a composition and contributes so valuably to the harmony of a picture as a whole.

## Interlude

Here is an excellent opportunity to engage in another project. As we have already discussed, it is not always wise to continue with one activity from the start right through to the end. This does not mean you should engage in another *at the same time*, because the mind can only focus on one thing at a time. The advice to engage in several projects *concurrently* really intends you to stage deliberate rests between activities.

In this chapter you might like to start another version of the plumbago, perhaps one which is much smaller, for example the size of our poppy project. Or you could start another project altogether; for example you could move to the next chapter and start the collage stage of the honeysuckle project (see p 48), where the procedure for the collage stage is the same as in this one.

For the time being, probably just one other completely different project will suffice; nevertheless, note that I am currently engaged on four or five projects, and not one of them is yet finished. They are all helping each other to grow together. With one or two I have encountered immense problems, so that I am almost tempted to wish I had never started them! Yet if we can stand back and try to see things objectively, we often learn more from such difficulties than from simple successes. Indeed, if we are concerned to explore and experiment, then we must accept that difficulties and problems are bound to exist, and can only help us grow in our creative development. Not only should we accept them, but welcome them gladly!

PLATE 21 shows another version of plumbago, in which the approach to the start of the collage was slightly different. The original guide for this panel was a painting of the plumbago set against the conservatory door. The vertical proportions of the door jambs, moulding and panes of glass are indicated by vertical pieces and strips of various materials; these were sewn onto a hessian background. The piece on the extreme left was a length of sumptuous black-and-gold brocade which I had been longing to use for about twenty-five years, yet had never quite found the right use for until now. Otherwise the collage and embroidery methods entail the same procedure as the one in which we were presently engaged. However, I should mention that the double and rather solid thickness of the background fabric made subsequent hand-sewing very difficult. I almost had to use a pair of pliers to pull the needle through!

### Machine Embroidery

For this stage of the project you will need the following:

1 Your fabric collage (or collages) of plumbago

2 A range of machine sewing and embroidery threads in the following colours

   *a) pale oranges, yellows, pale browns (beiges and fawns)*

   *b) pale violets, purples and greys*

   *c) pale to dark greens in hues ranging from yellow-greens to blue-greens*

   *d) pale to mid-toned blues of that hue which is within the purple-blue range, such as ultramarine and royal blues.*

3 A sewing machine which will either 'drop' or 'cover' its 'feed'

4 A darning foot

5 A tailor-tacking foot or a fringe foot

My advice is to start with those pieces within the picture which are the smallest. In mine, these appear to be the most pronounced and the most important, namely the white and blue pieces of fabric which represented the flower clusters. We placed them carefully at the collage stage, now we must secure them early at this sewing stage.

Let us begin with a white thread. Remember that it is as well to have the same colour below on the spool as is threaded through the machine above. The method and procedure for sewing at this stage are the same as for the poppies: to remind you, clip on the darning foot, insert a fairly thick needle (size round about 90 or 100), drop or cover the feed, set the stitch-width to the widest zigzag, and set the stitch-length to the 'still' position as this saves unnecessary wear and tear.

Now, sew over and across all the white fabric with this white thread; remember that it helps to unify and integrate the design if you can take this thread elsewhere in the picture where appropriate. Stay with the same guidelines as before: that is, for ninety per cent of the area within the picture, match the self-same colour and tone. In this instance, put white on white. For five per cent, put this thread on any other colour within the picture so long as it is nearly the same tone: for example, you could take a little of this white thread over the very pale green and yellow fabric. For the remaining five per cent it may be possible to allow the thread to travel across fabric of any colour and any tone; however, remember that it is *only* five per cent.

Continue in this manner with each one of your coloured threads in turn so that all your pieces of fabric are secure. Compare PLATE 22, which shows the completion of this stage of the machining, with PLATE 20 which shows the end of the former collage stage, and notice how the picture is much more integrated.

If you are working on two pieces concurrently, put this embroidery to one side now, and start sewing on your second collage. If you are not, I urge you to put this way of working into practice soon, because you need to have a rest, and you should allow your picture also to have a rest. Put it away for a day or two and bring it out later so that you may make a clearer assessment of how the balance and harmony of your design is progressing. Looking at a piece from a distance in space as well as time, even holding it up in a mirror, will help us to see what we are doing in an objective manner.

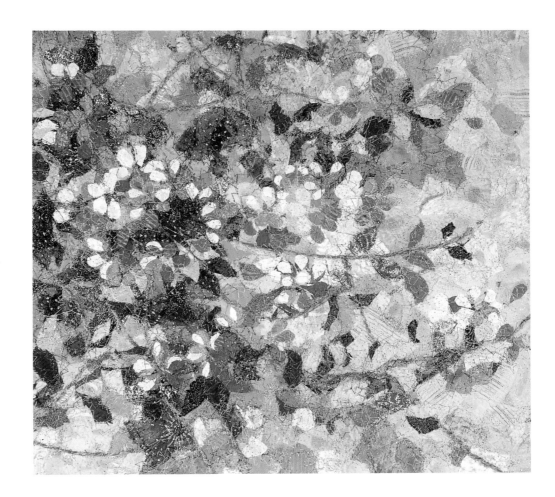

*Plate 22*
COMPLETION OF THE FIRST
STAGE OF MACHINE EMBROIDERY

*Plate 23*
COMPLETION OF THE HAND-
EMBROIDERY STAGE

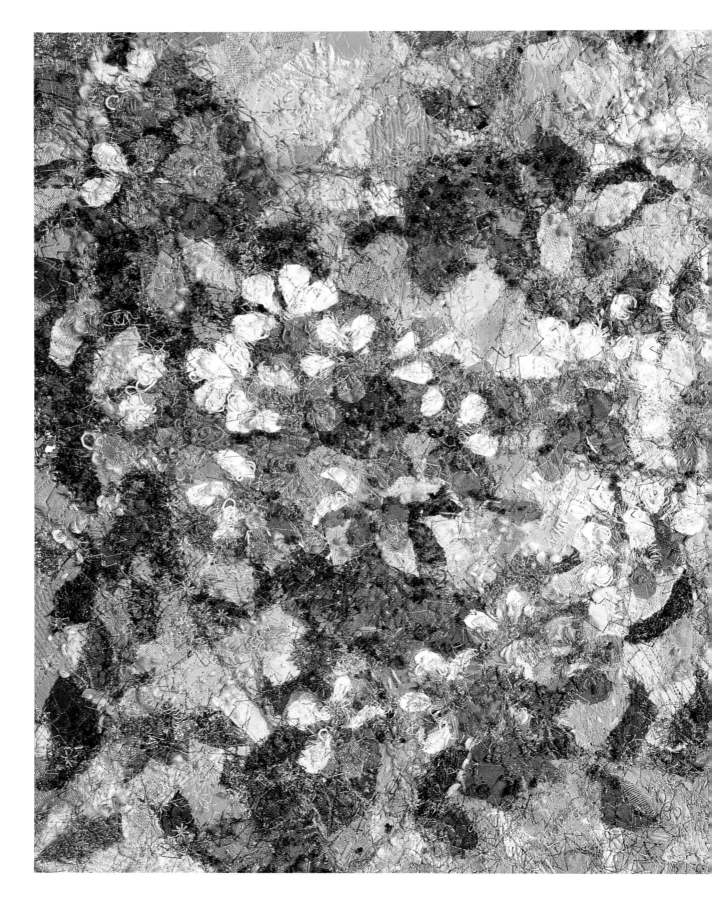

### Hand Embroidery

At this point we shall employ a different technique. Often a significant difference may be achieved in another project by making just one change in a number of constancies.

Thus, rather than using straight stitch as for the poppies, we shall use what I call 'looped stitch', which is a short stitch where the needle is inserted close behind where it has just emerged, and is not completely pulled through. This method not only produces a loop, but it also secures the stitch because the underneath thread is penetrated by virtue of the backward direction of the stitch.

PLATE 23 shows how looped stitch has been employed in the areas representing the flowers and the leaves. These were made with a range of different tones of blue and white for the blossoms, and various tones and hues of green for the leaves. Contrasting textures of threads were chosen deliberately so that the matt threads matched similar fabric and contrasted with shiny fabric. Likewise, glittering threads matched the shiny and contrasted with the matt fabrics.

Looped stitch enhances the texture of the surface considerably, and brings the panel into the third dimension: it is as if a relief-sculptured panel were being made, only it is soft rather than hard.

However, by putting such loops only in the areas which portray the leaves and the blossoms, the rest of the picture looked neglected—I wanted to emphasise these features, but not at the expense of making them look separate from the rest.

The solution was to embroider them with much smaller or lower loops. These were made with thinner threads, and many stitches were pulled quite close to the fabric so that they actually became what are known as 'seed' stitches.

*Plate 24*
COMPLETION OF THE PLUMBAGO
PROJECT, 1991

*Plate 25*
DELHI SHAWL. HAND
EMBROIDERY USING FLOSS SILK
AND STRAIGHT STITCHING.
NOTICE THE VIBRANT EFFECT OF
JUXTAPOSING THE
COMPLEMENTARY COLOURS RED
AND GREEN
(*HALL-TOWNLEY COLLECTION*)

## Conclusion

PLATE 24 shows the completed embroidery panel. For the final stage, take the embroidery back to the sewing machine (we did the same with the poppy project). We shall use a stitch that will match the loops we have made by hand at the previous stage.

Clip on the tailor-tacking or fringe foot. The feed on the machine needs to be in operation, so either bring it up or uncover it (depending upon your particular machine). Set the needle setting either to the right or to the left: the process begins and ends with a close straight stitch, and for the duration proceeds with a zigzag stitch of variable lengths. You may need to loosen the top tension slightly. Choose a colour you wish to begin with, and match top and bottom threads.

If you have never used this foot before, you may like to practise on spare material. Start with a straight stitch which is close in length for six or seven stitches. Bring the needle out of the fabric and set the stitch-width to the widest zigzag; try a few stitches by moving the wheel by hand so that you can see that the needle is clearing the flange of your foot and that the tension is correct. Then proceed normally. You will see that the loops, which are formed by the thread being raised by the flange of the foot, fall off the back and create an amazing effect.

It may amuse you to know that when I first discovered what this foot could do, I got so carried away that I completely covered my picture so that it ended up looking like a towel! So, try to vary the stitch length as much as possible as this will help to relieve what might become too repetitive. Follow the same guidelines as before: for ninety per cent of the area put a close stitch on the same colour and tone of material, and for the remaining ten per cent open up the stitch-length for travelling over other colours and tones of material. When you are finished with each coloured thread, try to remember to end with six or seven straight stitches; these will secure the loops which otherwise would sink.

Once again I hope you are content with what you are doing, pleased with what you have discovered, and happy to continue with our next project.

***Plate 26***
'LACE-CAP HYDRANGEAS'
(DETAIL), DESIGNED AND
WORKED BY EIRIAN SHORT,
1990, USING STRAIGHT STITCH
LIKE BRUSH STROKES.
SOMETIMES THREE DIFFERENT
STRANDS OF CREWELWOOL ARE
BLENDED TOGETHER IN THE
NEEDLE.

NOTICE HOW THE BLUE
COLOURS ARE MADE PROMINENT
BY THE VARIETY OF DIFFERENT
HUES USED, THE EXPANSIVE
TONAL RANGE, AND BY THE
VESTIGES OF YELLOW AND PALE
ORANGE (BLUE'S
COMPLEMENTARY) IN THE
SURROUNDING AREAS
(*PHOTOGRAPH: EIRIAN SHORT*)

# ℋONEYSUCKLE

FROM: *A MIDSUMMER NIGHT'S DREAM*

*I know a bank whereon the wild thyme blows,*
*Where oxlips and the nodding violet grows*
*Quite over-canopied with luscious woodbine,*
*With sweet musk-roses, and with eglantine:*
*There sleeps Titania some time of the night,*
*Lull'd in these flowers with dances and delight . . .*

WILLIAM SHAKESPEARE

*Plate 27*
'HONEYSUCKLE'. OIL PAINTING,
1991

The very name 'honeysuckle' implies an abundance of honey for the bee; as John Keats wrote '. . . and honeysuckles full of clear bee-wine'. Very sweetly scented, this flower's perfume can be detected from far away, especially in the early evening when it has been basking all day long in the hot summer sun. Often growing in the wild, it can transform its surroundings into a place of real enchantment. The one in my garden climbs and creeps all over the place, thus manifesting its other name, the woodbine. In fact I have encouraged it to entwine its many tendrils along the pergola, through the trellises and around the trunks of trees.

### The Pattern

This project is planned to progress naturally and easily from both the poppy and the plumbago projects. The overall approach and procedure is just as it was before, so you may consolidate your understanding. However, there will be some new variations in technique and in interpretation so your knowledge will develop ever forwards.

PLATE 27 is a recent painting of the honeysuckle in my garden, and I have chosen a small part from the top right-hand corner as the guide for this project. I thought it wise to select just a small section because the flower blooms are rather complicated, and as this is still only our third project, it is important not to be too ambitious. Moreover, because the individual parts of the honeysuckle flowers taper so gracefully we shall need to do some very careful cutting and

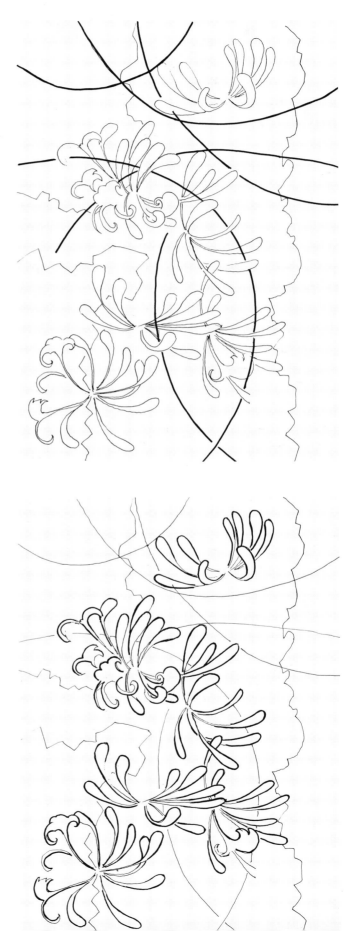

sewing, which might become rather too exacting and exhausting if there were too many to do. Follow my design, or draw out your own design from another picture of honeysuckle.

The size of my pattern is approximately 200 × 300 mm (8 × 12in)—you will need to enlarge to this. To help our procedure to flow easily, it would be as well to have three copies: one each for the areas which represent the wall, for the stems, and for the flowers (see Figs 6, 7, 8, page 48/49).

As a rule, the flower parts of the honeysuckle curve upwards as if they are smiling, sometimes tilting themselves to one side allowing the upper parts of the blooms to curve downwards. This complementary play of curves is repeated in the way the stems and the leaves swing in different directions. We can exploit all this, and so make a deliberately rich interplay of curves which gently twist and turn, encouraging the eye to follow their graceful convolutions throughout the entire composition.

It is for such reasons of harmonic necessity that we should avoid copying the picture exactly. Remember that the picture and the pattern are there to use as guide and helpmate, and *not* as task-master! Some people refer to this as artistic licence, though I would rather call it artistic necessity!

Look at PLATE 28: it is a detail of a panel designed by William Morris which forms part of the collection of the Embroiderers' Guild. We may not be able to detect quite what flower has been depicted because it is so stylised. However, what is infinitely more important is how every single stitch seems to fit and flow into the design and is everywhere a crucial part of the entire configuration.

> *That each part has its own particular arrangement is not enough; they must all agree together and make but one harmonious whole.*
>
> ROGER DE PILES

### Selecting the Fabrics

If possible use either green or brown hessian for your backing fabric. Cut it slightly larger than the intended picture size, as before, a margin of about 50 to 75mm (2 to 3in) will be sufficient. Do not worry if you have neither of these colours because whatever colour you have remember that it is possible to use any colour because the collage pieces can be made to cover the background completely.

For the collage, select blacks, browns and very dark greens to represent the areas of the wall and distant leaves lurking in shadow. Find some mid- to pale-toned greens for the nearer leaves, and a variety of yellows, whites and very pale reds and yellows for the flowers. As always, choose a number of hues of all these colours and select a range of various textures. Because the background wall is very dark, I have dared to use a lot of shiny and glittering fabrics, some of which have sequins already sewn into the material. This will help to portray reflected light in the darkly shadowed passages of the composition.

If your rag-bag is getting low you can top it up in a number of ways without it costing you very much. I started by purchasing secondhand garments, old bedspreads and curtains from charity shops and jumble sales. Very often tailors', dressmakers' and upholstery shops will give away their off-cuts and swatches of material. One of my suppliers is an Indian garment-making establishment whose materials are wonderfully lavish and splendid!

### *The Fabric Collage*

Start your project feeling relaxed, with the right equipment to hand. You will need:

1. Yourself, seated in a comfortable upright chair facing a clear working surface, and feeling calm and contented
2. The backing fabric placed on the surface in front of you and your fabric scraps arranged in the following groups:
   *a) dark browns, dark greens and blacks*
   *b) mid- to pale-toned greens*
   *c) pale reds, pale oranges, yellows and whites*

3. A pair of paper scissors and another pair for cutting the fabric
4. Three copies of the paper pattern
5. A small brush
6. A pot of PVA adhesive
7. Some green and brown yarns
8. The honeysuckle picture

We shall start with the area which represents the wall. Use the pattern which shows the distinction between the dark brown and the dark green as a guide (Fig 6). Cut the fabric of these colours in a fairly random manner: some very small and others slightly larger, some straight and others curved. Remember

*Plate 29*
COMPLETION OF THE COLLAGE
STAGE

that balanced harmony can be achieved by repetition and by contrast in *everything* that we do. Assemble these pieces and secure them with the adhesive to the background fabric as the pattern indicates. On my own collage I added some small pieces of black machine lace and some navy-blue gauze at this stage. Using diaphanous fabrics in this way helps to unite the design at a very early stage and can be usefully employed in all projects done in this method.

Next, position the stems with the green and brown yarns; it is helpful to place these as soon as possible because it establishes the rhythm of the design early on. As before, fix them with the adhesive and use the next copy of the paper pattern (Fig 7) to ensure their correct position. If, for the balance of the design, you wish to put a few more in, or leave some out, then do so; always rely on your instinctive judgement in such things.

I found that it was not necessary to use the paper pattern for positioning the flowers (though if this alarms you, continue to use it as your guide). I looked directly at the painting for guidance with the flower blooms, and cut each individual part separately. I then assembled them as carefully as possible. PLATE 29 illustrates the collage completed at this stage. Notice that I left a lot of spaces, which eventually became the centre of each bloom; this is

*Plate 30*
COMPLETION OF THE FIRST PART
OF THE MACHINE EMBROIDERY
STAGE

because the junction is so fine and delicate that I decided to depict this part with stitching only and not with fabric, lest the line should appear thick and coarse, and altogether without grace.

Once you have completed this stage you might like to put it on one side and engage in another project of this flower; develop this second collage up to the same stage as the first one so that both are ready for the machine-embroidery stage. If you need to alter or amend the first one because your second one has given you some ideas, then do so at once. The transference of knowledge is one of the main reasons for working on two or more pieces concurrently. PLATES 31 and 32 show two smaller versions of this procedure, and PLATE 34 a much larger interpretation with the addition of five thousand tiny beads for extra enrichment. This has amazed some people; but then, you only need patience for what you do *not* like to do!

### Machine Embroidery

For this stage you will need the following:

1 Your fabric collage (or collages) of honeysuckle
2 A range of machine sewing and embroidery threads in the following colours:
   *a) blacks, browns and dark greens*
   *b) mid- to pale-toned greens*
   *c) pale reds, pale oranges, yellows and whites*
   You could also include metallic threads in all these colours.
3 A sewing machine which will either 'drop' or 'cover' its 'feed'
4 A darning foot
5 An embroidery foot or a presser foot

We shall begin with the same method of machine-sewing as we used in our last two projects. So, clip on the darning foot; insert a fairly thick needle, size round about 90 or 100; drop or cover the feed according to the instruction manual for your machine; set the stitch-width to the widest zigzag, and set the stitch-length to the 'still' position.

Let us begin with the flower parts; they are so fine and delicate that we need to sew them now before

their edges begin to fray. Using the pale-red, pale-orange, yellow and white threads sparingly and in turn, embroider freely over all these parts until each piece of fabric is secure. Continue in this manner with the various green and brown threads at your disposal until all pieces of fabric are sewn to the background material.

The next stage of machine-sewing is quite different from anything that we have attempted before. The plan is to define some of the contours such as the stems and, most particularly, the edges of the flowers: to do this, bring the feed up (or uncover it) and replace the darning foot with the embroidery foot (otherwise use the presser foot, the one normally used for straightforward sewing). Set the stitch-length so that the stitches will be very close together; during the operation you could also vary the density very slightly so that some of your edges may be as close as satin stitch. This will avoid too much repetition. Even more important is the stitch-*width*: this will be varied continually in order to delineate the tapering curves. Have a look at PLATE 30 to see what I mean.

I suggest you start at the centre of each bloom with a straight stitch, aim for one particular petal and sew carefully. As you reach the petal, guide the material with your left hand and gradually open up the width of the stitches with your right hand as you sew around the edge. You could go all the way round the petal with this thread. If you do, come back to your initial starting-point and taper the stitch-width so that you finish with a straight stitch; then aim for another petal.

This time you may decide to go only half-way round with this thread, and continue with another thread later on. If you decide to do this, still taper the stitch-width gradually so that you finish eloquently rather than suddenly. Clumsy and awkward effects must be avoided at all costs because our aim is to portray the elegance and grace of the honeysuckle.

To begin with this is not easy, so practise on a spare piece of material. In a short time you will be surprisingly proficient! Continue in this manner with other coloured threads until all the edges of the flowers are clearly delineated with a multitude of different yellows, pale reds, pale oranges and whites.

**Plates 31 and 32**
TWO SMALL VARIATIONS ON THE
HONEYSUCKLE PROJECT, 1992

Plate 33
COMPLETION OF THE
HONEYSUCKLE PROJECT,
1992

## Conclusion

Our aim is to create a jewel-like intensity! Therefore the final stage includes a little hand-stitching and a little more machine embroidery.

Although the close machine-stitching will have clarified the line of the honeysuckle flowers, it will also have flattened the surface of the picture. In order to bring some parts out into relief, I outlined some of the edges of the flowers with pale-red and gold threads; and to ensure their correct position, I employed a useful technique known as couching. To do this effectively the threads which are to be couched should be held firmly and not allowed to loop or pucker. It is also important to ensure that the couching-down stitch is firm and taut.

The final stage of this our third project is to return the embroidery to the sewing machine and embellish the entire surface with one of its set patterns (remember the jewel-like intensity!). Choose one which you think is attractive. The Pfaff sewing machine makes a tiny flower which I particularly like, and I have repeated this pattern in three different threads. Look at PLATE 33 to see the result. Notice that the metallic brown and purple threads are almost imperceptible because for most of the time I placed them only on fabric of similar tones and colours; the variegated green thread is more noticeable, however, because it is set against slightly

same subject has been interpreted in a completely different way. I have already indicated how delicate and intricate is the honeysuckle; the way it entangles and entwists itself is amazingly graceful. In our fabric collage projects, and particularly their subsequent embellishment with machine and hand embroidery, we have been able to do honour to the honeysuckle's glorious colour, and perhaps to evoke its delicious perfume by our use of sumptuous fabrics. However, although refinement and delicacy of line have been attempted, these have not really been fulfilled.

The illustrations (PLATES 35 and 36) show my attempts to interpret another section of the original source (the oil painting of honeysuckle as in PLATE 27). They are created entirely and only with machine-stitching. Furthermore, they have been made with only one stitch. I set the sewing machine to a straight stitch, lowered the feed, used no foot at all, and stapled the fabric to a home-made embroidery frame made from plywood, its inner dimensions approximately 220 × 255mm (9 × 10in.) This is an amazing way of making an embroidery hoop, and one which is larger than any I know to be available commercially. It means we can embroider the entire picture without having to keep moving the fabric from one position in the frame to another.

The first illustration (PLATE 35) shows the beginning stages. Start by drawing, with a soft pencil or a fine felt-tipped pen, the main contours of the design on to the background fabric; I used a mid-toned brown silk material. Beginning with a white thread I followed the curving lines with the straight stitch. I progressed to the navy blue, and then on to the greens, and each time followed my drawn lines. I also had the oil painting propped up on a chair next to me, so I could always refer to it. As with our previous projects, I found it necessary to match top and bottom threads. The illustration shows, even at this early stage, that the design is developing as a whole. Although by no means finished, it could be described as complete at this stage of development.

The second illustration (PLATE 36) shows the embroidery both complete and finished. I followed exactly the same procedure and the same sequence of coloured threads to begin with; pale reds, pale oranges and yellows followed, then more greens

different tones and colours; yet it is comparatively muted in relation to the contrast between the very pale flowers with their very dark surroundings. Remember to use the same guide for matching threads with fabrics as in the previous projects. Namely: ninety per cent: self-same colour and tone; five per cent: same tone, but other colours; and the last five per cent: other colours and other tones. In this way you will discover that you can embellish your embroidery quite lavishly without fear of making such decorations intrusive or vulgar. On the contrary, your result will be absolutely resplendent.

## Drawing with the Needle

There is another way of interpreting our honey-suckle design: look at PLATES 35 and 36 to see how the

(OPPOSITE) *Plate 35*
FIRST STAGE OF 'DRAWING WITH
THE NEEDLE'

*Plate 36* (RIGHT)
COMPLETION OF 'DRAWING
WITH THE NEEDLE' (DETAIL):
'HONEYSUCKLE', MACHINE
EMBROIDERY, 1992

and blues, and eventually finishing with white. I included metallic threads in gold and silver, also in greens and blues, and one very attractive thread which is both purple and green which was particularly useful in enlivening the shadowed areas.

Rather than the same brown silk material which I used for the unfinished example, I chose a rich brocade, also brown but with a bias towards orange. As well as being guided by the original painting I was also influenced by the pattern of the brocade. It is important to be guided by the nature of the flowers which we are interpreting, but we should also be guided by the nature of the materials themselves.

About half-way through this project, I noticed that my threads were breaking a lot. I adjusted tensions, thought that I was not threading up the machine correctly, checked the spool underneath, and forgot one of the most obvious reasons. My needle was blunt! Thus, do not be afraid to change your machine needles regularly, particularly if you do a lot of machine embroidery.

I hope you enjoyed doing this little project. There will be more opportunities to practise and consolidate this technique in different ways and with different flowers. Our next flowers also twist and twine, but in other respects they are quite different.

# CLEMATIS AND WISTERIA

## FLOWERS

*Yes; there is heaven about you; in your breath*
*And hues it dwells. The stars of heaven ye shine;*
*Bright strangers in a land of sin and death,*
*That talk of God, and point to realms divine ...*

*Ye speak of frail humanity; ye tell*
*How man, like you, shall flourish and shall fall:-*
*But ah! ye speak of Heavenly Love as well,*
*And say, the God of flowers is God of all ...*

*Sweet flowers, sweet flowers! the rich exuberance*
*Of Nature's heart in her propitious hours:*
*When glad emotions in her bosom dance*
*She vents her happiness in laughing flowers ...*

*Childhood and you are playmates; matching well*
*Your sunny cheeks, and mingling fragrant breath:-*
*Ye help young Love his faltering tale to tell;*
*Ye scatter sweetness o'er the bed of Death.*

HENRY FRANCIS LYTE

*Plate 37*
CLEMATIS MONTANA. OIL
PAINTING, 1991

I have chosen two other climbing plants for our next endeavours because they seem to follow on naturally from those in the previous chapters. The first is the clematis which creeps and climbs, twists and twines rather like the honeysuckle, though in other respects it is quite different. The second is the wisteria, also a climber and a longer-living one; it, too, is quite different in character and personality. The reason for grouping the clematis and the wisteria together is simply because these particular varieties consist of various hues of violet.

The methods, procedure and techniques for all the projects in this chapter are variations of those in which we have engaged before. Therefore it will not be necessary to explain all of them again in detail, and I shall simply refer you to the relevant, previous passages in order to refresh your memory. Here again is an opportunity to practise, to consolidate your understanding and to refine and broaden your knowledge. We shall investigate new ways of interpretation, new colour combinations and the use of line and tonal distributions. These are all essential ingredients which contribute to creating a balanced harmony in our compositions.

There are six projects in this chapter, four inspired by the clematis and two by the wisteria. Try to work on two or more projects concurrently so that you give yourself the chance to learn from each of them and to transfer your knowledge quickly and easily.

# THE CLEMATIS

In the country the wild clematis is known as 'hedgevine' or 'traveller's joy' and is purported to signify mental beauty. After it has flowered it turns to white gossamer-like tufts and is then called 'old man's beard' or 'grandfather's whiskers'. Some people call it 'lovebind', thus referring to the way it clings in loving embrace to other plants, creating curious interlacements. Indeed, its propensity to twist and twine itself around other growing things prompted the ancient Greeks to call it *klema* because it

resembled the vine. Some poets have described it as the 'virgin's bower' because of the way it trails over trellises and arbours, making secret shaded places for shy young ladies into which they may retreat, retire and rest.

### The First Clematis Project

PLATE 37 is one of a series of studies which I made of the *Clematis montana* which entwines itself amongst the winter jasmine and which together clamber over the porch around my front door. This particular *Clematis montana* is white, though you might not have thought so if you were to look at the colours which I had to use in order to represent my response to what I saw. Let us pause here to discuss this matter of colour perception a little further.

We need to ask ourselves whether we all see colours in the same way and whether the names we give to colours are helpful. I believe that we do *see* colours in the same way but that individuals have learnt to *identify* them differently. Blue and violet are a good example of two colours where the overlap can vary enormously depending on individual perception.

The term violet brings us to the question of whether the names we give to colours are helpful. Many of us use the term 'purple' rather than 'violet', although strictly speaking violet is the correct name, particularly when referring to the colour in the spectrum. Purple is a hue of violet with a bias towards red.

Another example which causes much argument is the cusp between blue and green. The term turquoise can be confusing as the semi-precious stones known as turquoise vary in colour between a definite green and a distinct blue. Let us try to sort it all out a little more clearly.

Fig 9 is a diagram illustrating the colour wheel which contains the six colours of the spectrum. It is now generally accepted that there are six main colour categories: red, orange, yellow, green, blue and violet; *not* included is the traditional seventh colour, indigo, which was once considered a distinct part of the spectrum. However, I understand from present-day authorities in physics that Isaac Newton,

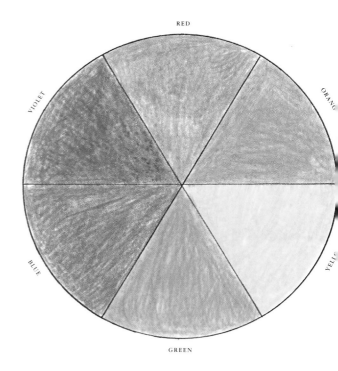

*Fig 9*
THE SIX-PART COLOUR WHEEL

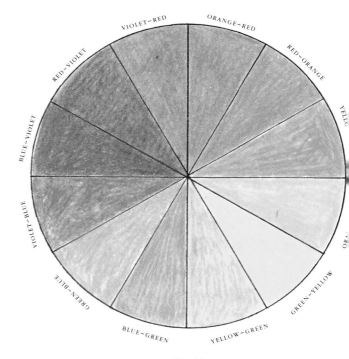

*Fig 10*
THE TWELVE-PART COLOUR WHEEL

who devised the system, was something of a mystic and therefore it was significant that the seventh was found and chosen from one of the many cusps available. In fact we would all agree that *more* than seven distinct hues of colour can be seen in a bright rainbow.

Nonetheless, despite its limitations, the six-part colour wheel is an extremely useful diagram to show the three primary colours: red, yellow, and blue. It also shows three secondary colours: orange, green, and violet, and their placement indicates how each secondary colour is made, namely by the two primaries positioned either side of it; thus orange is made from a mixture of red and yellow, violet from blue and red, and green is a combination of yellow and blue. Moreover, this diagram shows how colours which are opposite each other are understood as complementary pairs; thus red is complementary to green, as yellow is to violet, and blue is to orange.

However, although this diagram is useful it is not quite enough, because within each colour category there are many hues. Thus if we wanted to make a really bright violet, we would be disappointed if we used a greenish-blue and an orangey-red; in fact we would need a blue and a red with less yellow in them, and be more biased towards violet itself. Fig 10 is another diagram which shows two hues of each of the six main colours of the spectrum. Rather than using metaphorical equivalents to describe them, like 'lemon yellow', I have used the adjacent colour as the adjective, for example '*green* yellow'. As a term, '*lemon* yellow' is too vague because although the yellow colour of some lemons is close to the green category, that of a really ripe lemon is actually closer to the orange.

I hope this helps to clarify our thinking and subsequent practice as regards the perception and use of colour. However, there is another question, or rather phenomenon, that needs to be raised, that of 'simultaneous contrast': when the eye is exposed intensely to one colour for a little while, there is the sensation of the complementary colour appearing adjacently. It happened to me when I was painting the so-called 'white' *Clematis montana*, which came as quite a surprise with this particularly gentle and delicate flower. First of all it was a revelation to realise that the white *Clematis montana* was not really white, but a very pale yellow. It was also

surprising to observe that the petals which were not illuminated by the sunlight and were therefore in shadow, were of a *violet* hue rather than the expected grey.

Now, here is a very useful exercise which you might like to try. Find all the white fabrics in your rag-bag. Put them in a heap to start with, and then sort them into smaller sub-divisions, the colour category of these determined according to which of the six main colours of the spectrum the white of each fabric is nearest. Some will appear very obviously biased towards one colour in particular, whereas others will not be so evident. However, I suspect few, if any, will appear 'pure' white. Try this exercise with other 'neutral' colours like greys and browns, and even blacks! (see PLATE 38). As well as sorting out your rag-bag, it will help you to develop a heightened sensitivity to colour, and as such is an invaluable preparation for this project because we now need to select colours carefully: yellow-whites, pale violet-greys, pale violets and pale purples for the flowers; a range of greens for the leaves; and browns, blacks, dark blues and very dark violets and purples to represent the dark recesses of the porch.

The method, procedure and techniques are exactly the same as they were for the plumbago project; the piece is $610 \times 460$mm ($24 \times 18$in). We shall start by covering the background hessian fabric, which could be either dark blue or brown, with small pieces of material to represent the dark areas of the porch. However, we must avoid making it gloomy. I found it helpful to use a lot of metallic and glittering fabric so that some reflected light might enliven the shadows. Over these pieces we can assemble the small pieces of fabric to represent the leaves and flowers. Remember, too, the possible effects of diaphanous materials: when sorting and choosing the yellow-white fabric, I found some machine-made lace and discovered that if placed over some pale-violet material it created an effect of

(PAGE 69) *Plate 39*
CLEMATIS MONTANA. FABRIC COLLAGE, MACHINE AND HAND EMBROIDERY, 1992

*Plate 40*
CLEMATIS JACKMANII. OIL PAINTING, 1990

Richard Box
July 90

dappled sunshine. It was just what I needed! And in order to enrich and enhance this effect, the final stage of the whole project was to embroider many looped stitches both by machine and by hand. When you do this, proceed through the machine- and hand-embroidery stages as before. My completed version is illustrated by PLATE 39.

If anything occurs to you that is a variation of what we have done before, put it into practice immediately. Always be guided by your creative instinct!

### The Second Clematis Project

PLATE 40 shows an oil painting of the *Clematis jackmanii* and it acts as the stimulus for this next project (PLATE 41). The *Clematis jackmanii* and its dark majestic colour have always held a mysterious fascination for me, and scarcely a summer will pass without my either drawing or painting it. Of all the flowers I have ever painted or embroidered I have found it the most difficult to portray! I have to be very careful not to make the blooms too dark, particularly with fabric and thread, and in order to realise their light, airy and delicate forms, which contrast nicely with their dark tones, I have to remember to notice and perhaps to exaggerate the pale areas caught in the sunlight.

The methods, procedures and techniques are the same as for our first honeysuckle project, but with the added texture of very low, looped hand-stitches. As before, help yourself by making a paper pattern, select an appropriate range of fabrics, and then proceed through the collage and the machine- and hand-stitching stages. My assessment of the first clematis project is that although the effect of dappled sunlight has been realised, a clarity of edge has been lost. In this one I am therefore attempting to ensure clear contours by employing a varied use of satin stitch with the sewing machine. This second project is also 610 × 460mm (24 × 18in).

*Plate 41*
CLEMATIS JACKMANII. FABRIC
COLLAGE, MACHINE AND HAND
EMBROIDERY, 1992

*Plate 42* (RIGHT)
'CLEMATIS'. FABRIC COLLAGE,
MACHINE AND HAND
EMBROIDERY, 1992

*Plate 43* (OPPOSITE)
CLEMATIS JACKMANII. MACHINE
EMBROIDERY, 1992

All colours seem to have their own 'personality'. Wassily Kandinsky, one of the first abstract painters, described brown as 'Outwardly inaudible, but ringing of a powerful inner harmony', and purple or violet as '. . . having a morbid quality'. Sometimes I find this is so with manufactured goods like paint or fabrics, but not so in nature; and certainly not with the glorious *Clematis jackmanii*. One way to vitalise this colour in both painting and embroidery is to include the two primary components that make the colour.

Look very carefully at PLATE 40 and PLATE 41 and you should see vestiges of blue and red in both. Try this yourself and see if you can remember to carry this principle in other projects; thus for each secondary colour it is possible to include the two primaries from which it is composed.

### The Third Clematis Project

This project is much smaller than the first two, being about 200 × 280mm (8 × 11in) (see PLATE 42). My inclination was to do the second project again but on a much smaller scale, and also to return to the *Clematis montana*. However, I particularly liked the shape of the *Clematis jackmanii* bloom on the bottom right-hand side of the oil painting (PLATE 40), so the design is finally a composition of elements from both paintings.

Follow the same procedure, method and technique as for the first honeysuckle embroidery (see p 48), and let us have the same aim: to realise a jewel-like intensity. The little daisy-like pattern which meanders over the entire embroidery in order to embellish the surface is picked out in a very dark-green thread, also, though hardly noticeable, a mid-toned and variegated green, and in a white thread. Remember how important it is to match both the tones and colours of the threads with those of the fabric if understatement is required, which is what we need here. And imagine my delight when I also noticed, just by a thrilling chance, how this stitch made a wonderful representation of stamens. Some people can be very disparaging of set patterns on their sewing machines, which is a pity because it is possible to be just as creative with these as with anything else.

### The Fourth Clematis Project

For our last clematis project (PLATE 43) we return to the same method as our second honeysuckle project,

which I described as 'drawing with the needle' by means of the sewing machine (see p 60). There are times when we would like to represent a certain delicacy of detail which is precluded by the flamboyance of sumptuous fabrics and the exaggerated stitch techniques sometimes employed in our larger projects. So bring out your embroidery frame and remove the foot from the sewing machine. I used my home-made plywood frame and stapled a green brocade to it; as much as anything I enjoyed being guided by the patterns of the fabric and trying to reconcile them with the directions of the curves within the painting.

Let us return to the *Clematis jackmanii* and mark out our design onto the fabric. With the same colour in the spool as in the machine above, let us construct our 'drawing' with straight stitch, with each colour in turn. As with the second clematis project, try using reds and blues as component parts of violet and purple. The more we practise the more confident we become, and indeed the more skilled and proficient.

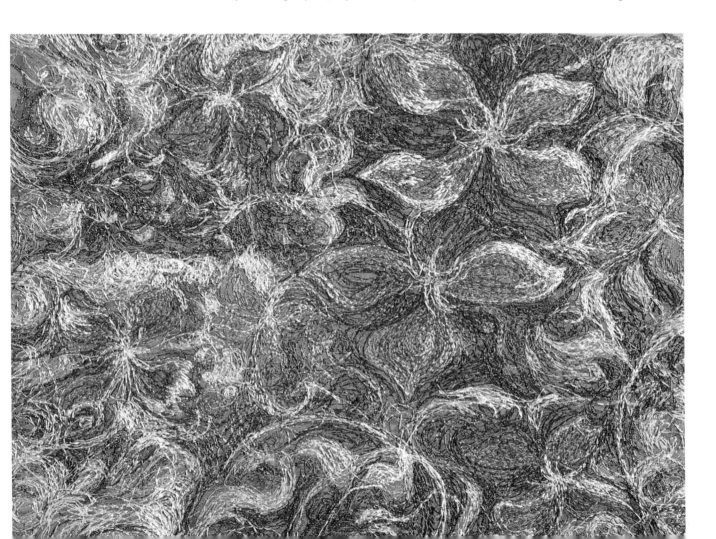

# THE WISTERIA

FROM: *WISTARIA TUSCAN*

*It has come, it has come again,*
*This lost blue world*
*That I have not seen for seven years,*
*And now there is no other earth beside it,*
*O what I have missed, these seven eyeless summers,*
*For this is a blue world shut into itself,*
*This trellis of wistaria, this blue fire falling;*
*Its leaves drop flame to every quarter of the winds,*
*But I lived seven years away and came not to it,*
*And now the flowers are sevenfold, their honey tongues*
*Loll like a million bells that quiver and don't ring,*
*Though the air all trembles and vibrates with them.*
*Then as now their blueness was alive*
*With quick spangled comedies, quick turncoat rain,*
*That fell by the trellis and was dyed in that colour;*
*There was never such a heaping; such a deep*
*piled fullness,*
*For the flowers lie on the pergola, like snow*
*disastered*
*From some whirling cataclysm thrown and tumbled.*

SACHEVERELL SITWELL

*Plate 44*
'WISTERIA'. OIL PAINTING, 1987

I have spent many joyful hours in the early summer months painting and drawing wisteria. The painting illustrated in PLATE 44 depicts a wisteria which has been well established for many years. It has been trained to form an arbour so that when it flowers you can sit almost 'inside' it, with its lusciously drooping blooms hanging all about like lanterns. On one occasion an extra delight was the song of blackbirds from deep within the interlacement of its branches, and the sight of them flying in and out with worms in their beaks to feed their young in a nest which they had built there.

### The First Wisteria Project

We shall follow similar methods, procedures and techniques as we did for the plumbago project and for the first clematis project, with one exception: there will be a different hand-embroidery stitch.

Choose a brown-coloured hessian. Cover this with small fragments of various brown fabrics and secure them with small specks of PVA adhesive. Using a paper pattern to guide you, assemble over these brown fragments even smaller pieces of green fabrics, cut into specific leaf-like shapes. Lastly, arrange the petals of the wisteria flowers; these are best cut out individually in pale-blue, pale-violet and purple hues, and white. Ensure that all these little pieces are secured with adhesive.

The next stage is, of course, machine-stitching. Use the darning foot and a thick needle, and lower the feed in order to embroider freely over the collage pieces with the appropriate coloured and toned threads until all are securely sewn on to the hessian background. For hand embroidery, try using small French knots instead of, or as well as, the looped stitch which we used in our earlier projects.

In conclusion, return the embroidery to the sewing machine and complete the picture with various densities of the machine looped stitch. Look at PLATE

*Plate 45*
'WISTERIA'. FABRIC COLLAGE,
MACHINE AND HAND
EMBROIDERY, 1990

*Plate 46*
'WISTERIA'. COLOURED PENCIL
DRAWING, 1992

45 to see my version of this completed project. The machine loops here are made with the Bernina sewing machine's tailor-tacking foot, and are much prouder and in higher relief than those made with the fringe foot belonging to the Pfaff sewing machine.

### The Second Wisteria Project

This is the last project in this chapter, and we shall have a third attempt at 'drawing with the needle', achieved by free machine embroidery; this method is first described in the second honeysuckle project (see p 60) and again in the fourth clematis project (see p 75).

PLATE 46 is a coloured pencil drawing of another wisteria in early bloom, just as the leaves are about to emerge, and it acts as our guide for this project. Choose a blue brocade whose hue is closer to violet than green, so that if any of its colour can be glimpsed through our embroidery stitches, it will form an appropriate component of the flowers' violet colour when in shadow.

Look at PLATE 47 to see the completed version of my attempt at this project. I followed the same procedure as before by drawing all the main colours of the design onto the brocade, and had the drawing by my side to act as a guide throughout the whole process. To be accurate, I even had to turn the drawing at the same time as I had to turn the embroidery for the needle to reach certain areas while it was in its home-made plywood frame. In fact the embroidery is slightly larger than the interior measurements of the frame, a perfectly solvable problem as long as I 'bent' one of my rules of procedure! I had to finish one part of the picture completely and then shift the fabric further down the frame, to start and complete the remainder of the picture at another 'sitting'. I found it was essential to put all the threads I used to one side and in the order I had used them in the first sitting, in readiness for the second sitting.

*Plate 47*
'WISTERIA'. MACHINE
EMBROIDERY, 1992

CHAPTER
FIVE

# Spring Flowers

## AND THE
## HERALDS OF
## SUMMER

FROM: *A Spring Morning*

*The Spring comes in with all her hues and smells,*
*In freshness breathing over hills and dells,*
*O'er woods where May her gorgeous drapery flings,*
*And meads washed fragrant by their*
*laughing springs.*
*Fresh are new opened flowers, untouched and free*
*From the rifling of the amorous bee.*
*The happy time of singing birds is come,*
*And Love's lone pilgrimage now finds a home;*
*Among the mossy oaks now coos the dove,*
*And the hoarse crow finds softer notes for love.*
*The foxes play around their dens, and bark*
*In joy's excess,'mid woodland shadows dark.*
*The flowers join lips below; the leaves above;*
*And every sound that meets the ear is Love.*

JOHN CLARE

*Plate 48*
'PRIMROSES, CELANDINES AND
VIOLETS'. COLOURED PENCIL
DRAWING, 1992

Primroses, violets, celandine, bluebells and apple blossom are some of the flowers that we associate typically with spring. Buttercups and daisies herald the coming of high summer. All these are found easily in our countryside; yet although they are common, at the same time they have a particular rarity in that each year they manifest new and special qualities. This is why I have grouped them together to inspire our next series of projects. Again, you will have opportunity to practise and consolidate, also to explore new elements and extend your knowledge; further, there are examples of traditional methods and techniques practised in innovative ways by experienced embroiderers.

# PRIMROSES

*Ask me why I send you here*
*This sweet Infanta of the year?*
*Ask me why I send to you*
*This primrose, thus bepearl'd with dew?*
*I will whisper to your ears:-*
*The sweets of love are mix'd with tears.*

*Ask me why this flower does show*
*So yellow-green and sickly too?*
*Ask me why the stalk is weak*
*And bending (yet it doth not break)?*
*I will answer:- These discover*
*What fainting hopes are in a lover.*

ROBERT HERRICK

The primrose always takes me by surprise. Suddenly in the middle of January this year, when least expected, one cheeky little bloom popped open and smiled down at me from a high bank in my garden. It was a reminder of what to expect when in April the raking sunbeams of early morning catch the tips of its petals all '. . . bepearl'd with dew'.

### The First Primrose Projec

PLATE 48 illustrates the coloured pencil drawing which will act as our guide for this project, portraying a cluster of primroses together with a few celandines and violets peeping out from amongst the shadows. We shall engage in our 'drawing with the needle' technique with the sewing machine to depict this scene; our first attempt at this was the second honeysuckle project (p 60) and our last the fourth clematis project (p 75). If you have other pictures of such flowers which you prefer, then choose from these; it is most important to be guided by what inspires you most. Also, if a pattern or such-like means your task is easier, then make one; or if you prefer, draw the main contours of the design onto a firm background material which you then put into an embroidery frame.

(PREVIOUS PAGE) *Plate 49*
'PRIMROSES, CELANDINES AND VIOLETS'. MACHINE EMBROIDERY, 1992
'THE SWEETNESS OF THE VIOLET'S DEEP BLUE EYES KISSED BY THE BREATH OF HEAVEN, SEEMS COLOUR'D BY ITS SKIES.'
*BYRON*

*Plate 50*
'PRIMROSES'. FABRIC COLLAGE AND MACHINE EMBROIDERY, 1990
'MY PRYMROSE IS THE LADY OF THE SPRINGE,
THE LOVELY FLOWER THAT FIRST DOTH SHOW HER FACE;
WHOSE WORTHY PRAYSE THE PRYTTY BYRDS DO SYNG;
WHOSE PRESENCE SWETE THE WINTER'S COLD DOTH CHASE.'
FROM: *THE GARDEN PLOT*

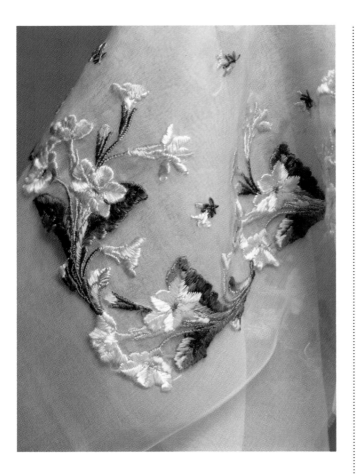

*Plate 51*
PRIMROSE HANDKERCHIEF.
EARLY TWENTIETH-CENTURY
SCHIFFLI MACHINE EMBROIDERY
IN SILK FLOSS THREADS ON SILK
CHIFFON
*(HALL-TOWNLEY COLLECTION)*

PLATE 49 shows my attempt at this project: I used a green brocade fabric which was stapled to my home-made plywood frame. Use as many different hues of the appropriate colours as you like. It is also interesting to use different types of thread ranging from matt to shiny, and if you are attracted to metallic threads, try using them as well. Try not to be too despondent if at first they break; all that is probably required is a slight change in either the top or the bottom tension on your sewing machine, or a change of needle, because after a good six to ten hours of use it will probably have become blunt.

See how you manage with this, and remember to have a rest half-way through by engaging in another project (which could well be the next one in this chapter), returning to this one later.

### The Second Primrose Project

Now we shall return to almost exactly the same procedures, methods and techniques as we employed for the poppy project, the very first in this book. As always, make a paper pattern to act as guide; gather together a range of different kinds of coloured fabric pieces; choose a firm backing fabric like green hessian; then start the collage process with tiny scraps of material, assembling each colour in turn so that you can watch the composition grow and develop as a whole.

Because you are becoming increasingly familiar with the technique, try to focus more attention on maintaining a balanced harmony throughout the entire operation. It helps always to repeat each of the elements, like a particular colour or the way a line curves, or a certain textural quality. You will remember that repetition is the agent which holds and binds the structure of the composition, whereas contrast invigorates it, giving it life and vitality. Therefore we now need to include complementary elements as well as repeating similarities.

Look at PLATE 50, which illustrates my completed version of this project, and you will see a number of contrasting and complementary elements. The various linking yellows which make up the primroses are emphasised by a small but important inclusion of violet and purple scraps of fabric in the shadows. The repeated curving lines which represent the stems and grasses, and the contours of the flowers and leaves, contrast themselves in both size and direction. The majority of matt fabric is complemented by a minor addition of glittering and shiny material. All such examples were planned, plotted and placed at the collage stage, so that the balanced harmony could direct similar operations with machine and hand embroidery.

Once you have completed the collage stage, take it to the sewing machine. Remember that it helps to work with a darning foot, if you want to work without a frame, so as to prevent the material puckering and threads snapping. Lower the feed and

start to free-embroider with a combination of zigzag and straight stitches until all your fabric pieces are secure. Do please remember that for most of the time you should match both colour and tone of the threads you use with the fabric on which they are sewn.

If you wish to embellish the surface further, try some straight stitching with a variety of hand-embroidery threads; use these to emphasise the dynamic flow of the grasses and to enhance the outward-reaching movement of the primroses' petals. Look again at PLATE 50, and you will see that I found it necessary to return the embroidery to the sewing machine to couch the hand-sewn threads with machine-stitching in order to unify the composition. See how you manage with this, trying to experiment as much as you like within the boundaries which this project allows.

*Plate 52*
PRIMROSE PURSE AND PINCUSHION 1991, DESIGNED AND WORKED BY MAUREEN KING USING TRADITIONAL STUMPWORK TECHNIQUES IN INNOVATIVE WAYS. THE MORE PROMINENT FLOWERS ARE RAISED BY MEANS OF SATIN STITCHING OVER PELMET VILENE. TWO BEADS ARE USED FOR THE CENTRE OF EACH FLOWER, THE OUTER BEAD BEING STITCHED OVER WITH PALE-GREEN SILK THREAD. DETACHED BUTTONHOLE STITCH FORMS THE STAMENS, THE CENTRE OF THE LEAVES AND THE STEMS OF THE FLOWERS. THE FLOWER ON THE PINCUSHION IS SURROUNDED WITH TINY GREEN BEADS, AND THE EDGES OF THE PURSE ARE TRIMMED WITH HAND-MADE BRAIDS AND TASSELS

# BLUEBELLS

## THE BLUEBELLS (EXTRACT)

*We stood upon the grass beside the road,*
*At a wood's fence, to look among the trees,*
*In windless noon the burning May-time glowed.*
*Gray, in young green, the beeches stood at ease.*
*Light speckled in the wood or left it dim:*
*There lay a blue in which no ship could swim.*
*Within whose peace no water ever flowed.*

*Within that pool no shadow ever showed;*
*Tideless was all that mystery of blue.*
*Out of eternities man never knew*
*A living growth man never reaped nor sowed*
*Snatched in the dim its fitness from the hour*
*A miracle unspeakable of flower*
*That tears in the heart's anguish answered to.*

*How paint it; how describe? None has the power.*
*It only had the power upon the soul*
*To consecrate the spirit and the hour,*
*To light to sudden rapture and console,*
*Its beauty called a truce; forgave; forgot*
*All the long horror of man's earthly lot,*
*A miracle unspeakable of flower*
*In a green May unutterably blue.*

JOHN MASEFIELD

*Plate 53*
'BLUEBELLS'. COLOURED PENCIL
DRAWING, 1992

### The Bluebell Project

Look at PLATE 53 and you will see a picture of a winding path through a sumptuous carpet of blue-bells. These grow in a woodland of birch trees near my home and demand a compulsory series of walks on April afternoons! The path is covered with the previous autumn's leaf-fall, and the leaves still maintain their glistening, rich brown colour with hues of orange and red, reminiscent of copper and old gold. Here is a stunning example of a pair of complementary colours: the orange and blue juxta-posed in this way vividly enhance each other.

The method used for this drawing is known as *cross-hatching*, where small groups of curved or straight parallel lines cross over each other. This technique allows the individual colours to remain distinct when inspected closely; yet when the draw-ing is viewed at a distance, the colours appear to mix and blend.

Let us try to emulate this method in our embroi-dery by 'drawing with the needle'; we have tried this already with the sewing machine, but this time there will be a slight difference in style and approach. In the drawing, the coloured pencils were used on white paper; therefore choose a plain white fabric for the surface which is to be stitched, and secure it to an embroidery frame. I used my home-made plywood frame, and because my project (illustrated in PLATE 54) was larger than the frame's internal measurements, I had to employ the same procedure as for the second wisteria project; I had to complete one half of the piece first and then move the fabric further along the frame in order to start and complete the remainder. Always do this if you want to make your embroidery larger than your frame; and re-member to keep all the threads you use, in the order in which you use them, so that continuity is kept flowing easily. Furthermore, in order to preserve this order, remember to shut the door to keep the cats out!

The stitching in PLATE 54 looks like a zigzag stitch but it is in fact a straight stitch. In order to emulate the cross-hatched lines which produced the draw-ing, I had my needle set to a straight stitch and

pushed the fabric backwards and forwards in short, even movements.

Try this method and see how you progress. It may well surprise you how even a slight change in style and approach can achieve quite a different effect.

# BLOSSOM

The months of April and May are particularly beloved of poets, when breezes are soft and skies are clear blue, and the sweetness and fragrance of flowering bushes and trees everywhere around fill the senses. It is a time when all is burgeoning in such profusion that we are almost spoilt for choice. I certainly had to discipline myself for this project, and choose just one bough from the crab-apple tree which grows at the bottom of my garden. PLATE 55 illustrates my drawing of a small part of the bough, and is our guide for our next embroidery.

## *The Blossom Project*

Follow my drawing for this project, or choose another picture of blossom from your own collection. I suggest that only a small part is used lest the design becomes too complicated; PLATE 56 shows how I have enlarged just the centre section of my drawing to use for the embroidery. There is so much subtlety in the slight changes of colour and tone within even one blossom that I was afraid I might negate such gentle qualities if I took on much more.

(LEFT) *Plate 54*
'BLUEBELLS'. MACHINE
EMBROIDERY, 1992

(BELOW) *Plate 55*
'CRAB APPLE BLOSSOM'.
COLOURED PENCIL DRAWING,
1992

(OVERLEAF) *Plate 56*
'CRAB APPLE BLOSSOM'.
FABRIC COLLAGE AND MACHINE
EMBROIDERY, 1992

Use the fabric collage and machine-embroidery method and remember it is always helpful to make a paper pattern to begin with. Select pale reds and white materials for the blossoms in sunlight, and mid-toned blues, greens, greys, violets and purples for the shadows in their petals. For the leaves in the foreground and in the distance, choose a variety of greens of many hues and some blues that are close to green. Remember that the inclusion of any primary colour which is a component of a secondary colour always seems to produce an invigorating effect.

Assemble these fabric pieces on to a green hessian backing material with the help of the paper pattern, in the way we have practised many times before. The repeating of a process not only helps to consolidate our understanding of what we are doing, it also reveals new possibilities and opens up new ways of interpretation. For example, my assessment of my picture at the completion of the fabric collage stage prompted me to do much more machine-stitching than I normally do at that stage. Moreover, rather than practising my usual zigzag stitching at this stage with this method, I decided to concentrate only on straight stitching in order to realise more subtle changes of colour and tone and a greater clarity of edge and contour. Look at PLATE 56 again and you will notice that I did not include any hand embroidery in this project because the composition seemed sufficiently resolved in its present condition.

Try this project, and see if you can discover and explore new ways of interpreting a familiar method.

# BUTTERCUPS

I wonder why it is that when we discover our lovely wild flowers in our garden beds we call them 'weeds' and snatch them out with venomous alacrity! Surely there must be some way of organising both wild and cultivated flowers to grow, if not in the same bed, at least in the same garden? Parts of my garden are cultivated and parts are kept for the wild flowers to flourish. During the months of April and May I can enjoy a procession of them, led by primroses, wild arum, windflowers, bluebells and stitchwort, swiftly followed by lady's smock, speedwell, cow parsley, vetch and buttercups.

PLATE 57 shows a watercolour painting of a splendidly swaying host of noble buttercups and acts as our guide for our next project.

### The Buttercup Project

We shall employ the 'drawing with the needle' method again with the sewing machine and with the addition of some hand embroidery. As always, we shall need to introduce one or two slightly different approaches into our now-familiar methods so that our experience is ever developing.

Attach a green brocade fabric to your embroidery frame. Draw the design on to the fabric so that you have a guide to show the needle where to travel. Remember to drop or cover the feed, work with a bare needle (without a foot), and keep to a straight stitch throughout. Use as many yellow and green threads as you like. It is possible to add further stimulus by using blue with the green, and also by putting dark violet and purple threads in the dark-green shadows near the yellow flowers. Being yellow's complementary colour, the violet and purple will enhance the flowers. Be sure to match the same dark tone of the violet and purple threads with those of the dark green, otherwise the desired effect will be lost.

About half-way through this machining process try including some hand-stitching. Once more, match colours and tones, so that your stitching embellishes the embroidery rather than intrudes upon it.

PLATE 58 is my attempt at this project. I used only two green threads, but spent several hours following and enhancing the straight machine-stitches with small long and short stitches. At first these appeared very different and almost alien to the design. However, by continued repetition the stitches started to become at one with the fabric and with the design as a whole. This teaches us that when only a few new elements are introduced they will often look strange until a few more are brought in to join them. Thus

*Plate 57*
'BUTTERCUPS'. WATERCOLOUR

Richard Box
May 1988

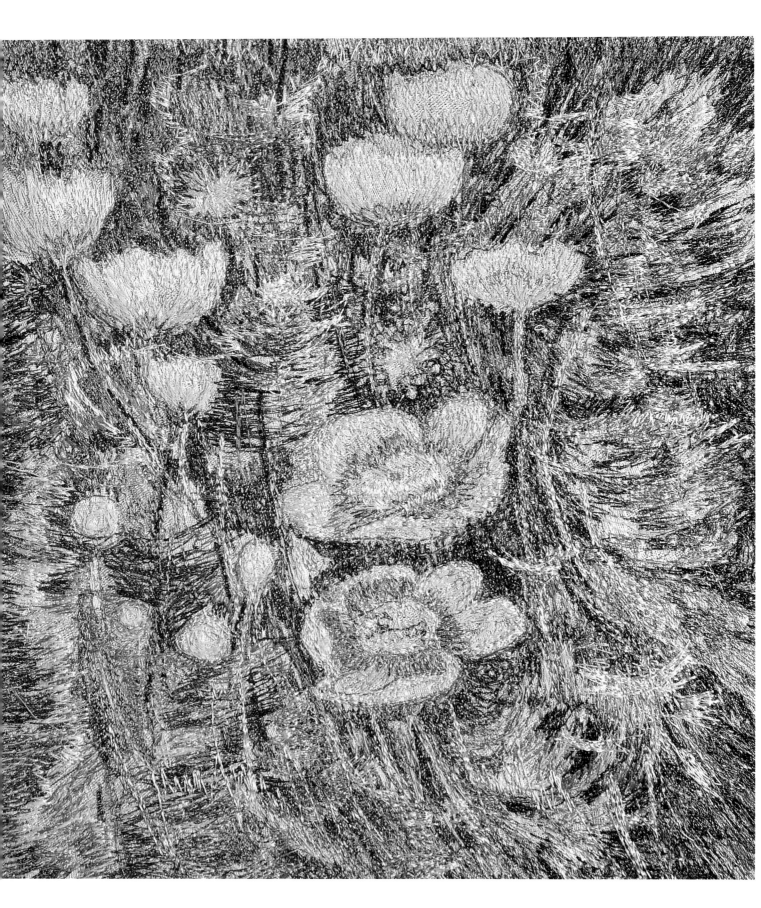

it is important to persevere with a project, and make an assessment *only* when a particular stage is complete, rather than at the start, and certainly not beforehand! Condemning an attempt before we even start only leads to inactivity and frustration, neither of which is creative!

The final stage is to return the embroidery to the sewing machine and to continue with free embroidery with the same straight stitching. Develop this as much as you like; you will find that your hand embroidery will be couched and will have become totally integrated with the design.

# DAISIES

A lawn studded with pink-tipped daisies is at once the despair of the gardener and a delight to ourselves. You can imagine what kind of lawn (if I dare to call it that!) I have in my garden. The daisy is quite true to its name: in the morning it opens its petals outwards and greets the sun as if it were the eye of the day; in the evening the petals fold over its centre like lashes in preparation to sleep.

A variety of daisy which I find particularly attractive is known as the ox-eye, or the moon daisy. During the months of May and early June they can be found growing in great profusion along the roadsides. The watercolour sketch illustrated in PLATE 59 was painted in a country lane in Buckinghamshire and is the guide for our next two projects.

### The First Daisy Project

Here is an opportunity for us to explore a traditional technique in an innovative way. You will see from PLATES 60 and 61 that the method used for this project is known as needlepoint, and the canvas worked with a single 'tent' stitch.

The innovative element is to use 'space-dyed'

wools. There are a number of such yarns available these days, in wool, silk and other substances, and they have enormous possibilities. The yarn is dyed in such a way that within quite a short length there are many colours and tones which subtly change. Examine PLATE 60 closely, and look at the areas in the lower part of the picture where I have begun to represent the stems; a number of hues and tones of green are seen to be present, but only one thread has been used.

Now examine PLATE 61 and look at the lower part again. Once more, only one thread has been used to construct the multi-coloured areas around the stems. It may not come as a surprise to you, now, to learn that only seven threads were used for the whole picture! Two plain yellows were employed to represent the centre of the daisies, a pure white for the petals in sunlight, and two other space-dyed wools for the petals in shadow, one consisting of a variety of very pale reds and greys and the other of pale blues and greys. Glance again at the watercolour

---

Plate 58
'BUTTERCUPS'. MACHINE
EMBROIDERY, 1992

*Fig 11*
PATTERN FOR THE FIRST AND
SECOND DAISY PROJECTS

illustrated in PLATE 59 to see how the grey shadows of the white petals have been represented by overlaying washes of pale red, pale blue and yellow. This is an interesting and colourful way to depict grey, and one which has been emulated in this needlepoint.

It is worthwhile pausing for a few minutes to elaborate this point. You will remember how we found all those subtle and very pale colour tints in our white fabric, and likewise the differences of coloured shades in our black fabric in our first clematis project. For our present purposes a little experiment will show how greys, blacks and browns can be made by mixing the three primary colours. This will help enormously in all the daisy projects, and many others besides.

Take up either coloured pencils or a paintbox, and choose one hue of each of the three primary colours: I suggest an orange-yellow, like gamboge or cadmium yellow; a violet-red like crimson or magenta; and a violet-blue like ultramarine or royal blue. If you are using pencils, overlay all three one on top of the other, being careful to press very lightly. You will find that you achieve the illusion of beige or fawn. And if you press harder with all three, browns and greys will emerge. As a general rule, if you want to produce brown add a little more red; if you want grey, add a little more blue; and to produce black, press very hard with all three pencils. If you are using paint, add lots of water at the start to produce the pale greys and browns, and less water for darker greys, browns and black.

Look again at PLATE 59 and particularly at the shadow of the daisies' petals: notice how from a distance these primary colours seem to merge and produce the illusion of grey.

If you decide to try this project, do please use the design which you see illustrated in Fig 11; it derives from the watercolour shown in PLATE 59 and was used to determine the colour zones on the canvas

(LEFT) *Plate 59*
'DAISIES'. WATERCOLOUR, 1991

*Plate 61* (RIGHT)
'DAISIES' THE COMPLETED
CANVASWORK EMBROIDERY, 1992

*Plate 60* (TOP RIGHT)
'DAISIES'. THE FIRST STAGE OF
CANVASWORK EMBROIDERY
USING SPACE-DYED WOOLS

before starting. Once you have done this you should find the whole process enjoyable and relaxing to do. Needlepoint is one of the most popular embroidery methods practised today, quite possibly because it is so soothing to do.

### The Second Daisy Project

For this project I have used the same watercolour as guide, as illustrated in PLATE 59, and it is particularly interesting to see how the same design can take on a completely different character if it is interpreted by another technique. Thus we shall try our 'drawing with the needle' method with the sewing machine, but, as with all our projects, there is a slight variation in our approach.

Attach some white fabric to your embroidery frame, remove the foot so that the needle is bare, set the needle setting to a straight stitch, and lower (or cover) your feed so that you are ready for free machine embroidery. Select a range of coloured threads such as yellows, greens and whites and try, once again, to depict the shadows in white by combining pale reds, pale blues and yellows.

Look at PLATE 62 and you will see that our embroidery will be constructed according to a technique known as 'granite stitch'. As the work is on white fabric, the design can be marked with coloured pencils so that we can see very clearly where the coloured threads are to be placed.

This time we will not follow the contours of the design, which is what we have done with all the previous projects in this method: we shall move the fabric in very small circular motions, so that whole areas are constructed with tiny overlapping circles. From a distance these circles merge and produce some unexpected textural effects and colour combinations.

Try this method and see how you enjoy it. At first, as with all new techniques, you may feel a little

*Plate 62*
'DAISIES'. MACHINE
EMBROIDERY USING THE
GRANITE-STITCH TECHNIQUE,
1992

### To The Daisy

*With little here to do or see*
*Of things that in the great world be,*
*Sweet Daisy! oft I talk to thee,*
*For thou art worthy:*
*Thou unassuming common-place*
*Of nature with that homely face,*
*And yet with something of a grace,*
*Which love makes for thee!*

WILLIAM WORDSWORTH

uneasy and awkward. However, as no doubt you have noticed when attempting other new methods, constant and regular practice helps to develop skills, and so confidence is gained. Always remember that our first concern is with adventure and experiment; any subsequent achievements are the fruits of our endeavours.

### The Third Daisy Project

Every year I try to make several studies of those gracefully tall specimens which flower in late July called Shasta daisies, and sometimes known as marguerites. PLATE 63 illustrates an oil painting which I made a few years ago in my garden. An extra delight to the scene was that in amongst the daisies grew a few brilliant blue cornflowers and some small wild marigolds. Behind this array it was possible to glimpse the bright orange of some Californian poppies and the violet-red hues of the phlox flowers which were growing in the distance. It is experiences such as this which continually fire the imagination and can act as an inspiration for many years to come!

PLATE 64 illustrates an embroidery of Shasta daisies, such as those in the painting. It is made by the fabric collage and machine and hand embroidery method that was first described for the plumbago project (p 32) and was developed in the first wisteria project (p 79). Try this method with these

*Plate 63*
'DAISIES'. OIL PAINTING, 1990

*Plate 64*
'DAISIES'. FABRIC COLLAGE,
MACHINE AND HAND
EMBROIDERY, 1990

flowers, and if any new variation or approach suggests itself to you, be brave enough to follow your creative instinct.

The most important lesson which I learned in the course of this embroidery was to avoid putting any shiny or glittering fabrics and threads in the lightest parts of the picture, such as the petals of the daisies in sunlight. I found that such fabrics and threads were *only* suitable for the shadowed areas, and to

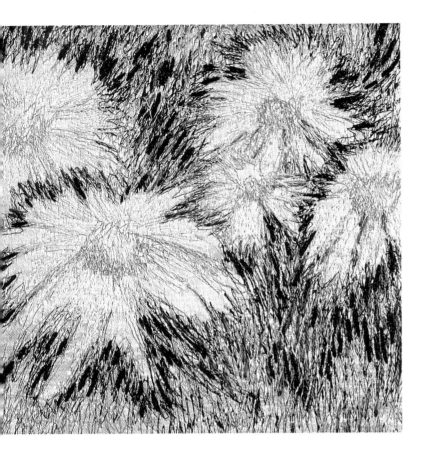

use *matt* fabrics and threads for the highlights. The reason for this is that although glittering and metallic fabrics and threads catch the light, they are also sometimes in shadow. Thus so, they appear dark and totally inappropriate when a constantly light passage is to be portrayed. However, sudden and unexpected gleams of light seen in shadows are quite acceptable and most welcome. You will see from the illustration that the palest petals of the daisies are made with matt white fabrics like cotton and linen; and the petals which are in shadow are made with some of the shiny and glittering metallic fabrics of the mid-toned colours in violet, purple, blue and green. This kind of colour accumulation, in conjunction with the sparkling fabric, imbues the shadows with movement and vitality.

You will remember that the final stage of this method is to embroider the surface with a series of looped stitches accomplished both by hand and by the sewing machine with the help of the tailor-tacking foot. This example has many more of these machine-loops than any of the previous projects: I decided to risk losing the clarity and crispness of the contours of the daisy petals in favour of a richly embellished and textured surface.

See how you manage this project yourself. Remember to take risks, because if we take care of the creative spirit, our progress will be all the more enjoyable!

### The Final Four Daisy Projects

Look at PLATES 65, 66, 67 and 68: you will see four small examples of daisies, all of which have been embroidered mainly in black and white. Each one is approximately 180mm (7in) square. You will have noticed that very often I make a number of studies of these flowers in pencil as well as in colour, and it occurred to me that it would be a challenge to see if it were possible to create an embroidery in monochrome and still make it interesting.

*Plates 65-68*
'DAISIES'. FOUR EXAMPLES OF
EMBROIDERY IN MAINLY BLACK
AND WHITE

The two on the right-hand side (PLATES 67 and 68) were machine- and hand-stitched by means of our 'drawing with the needle' technique. Grey threads as well as those in black and white were used, and also one in silver. For the reasons I have just mentioned (p 106), silver was used only in the parts depicting shadow.

The silver thread was too thick to use in the top of the machine, so it had to be wound onto a bobbin and placed into its case underneath. This meant I had to work the embroidery upsidedown! This is not as difficult as it sounds because I always match top and bottom threads; I then had a guide on the reverse side of the fabric which had been made by earlier sewing. Thus it was easy to direct where the silver was to travel.

Exactly the same procedure was used for the example on the top left (PLATE 65), although this time I used a wider range of black and white threads. In addition I used a particularly interesting range of threads which are not only metallised but also space-dyed at minute intervals in yellows, reds and blues, so that they appear grey from a distance. This is another example where we can experiment with a close mixture of primaries to create the illusion of grey.

These three examples were embroidered on white material. The fourth example, illustrated on the bottom left (PLATE 66), was embroidered on black fabric. The petals and stems were indicated first by applying silver and gold fabric to depict the shadowed parts, and matt white to represent the parts in sunlight. Zigzag machine-stitching first attached these pieces to the black backing fabric. Over this, looped stitches accomplished by both hand and machine softened the hardness of the contours and created a textured surface in comparatively high relief for such a small embroidery. The final stage was to sew the entire picture with tiny beads, silver, gold, black and white.

Try some of these monochrome exercises, and you will see just how much you enjoy them! You will also discover that if we exert a strict discipline upon ourselves, like limiting our range in this way, an unusually large number of unexpected opportunities often present themselves, thus extending the creative possibilities.

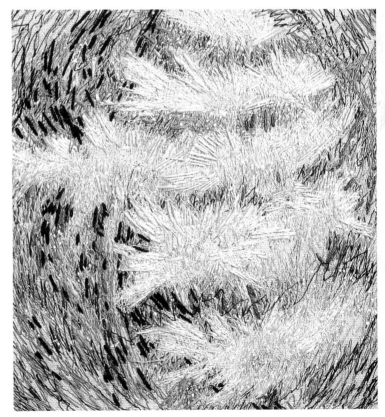

*Plate 69* (OPPOSITE)
'DAISIES, IN AN ART NOUVEAU
VASE', DESIGNED AND WORKED
BY EIRIAN SHORT, 1990, USING
STRAIGHT STITCH LIKE BRUSH
STROKES. SOMETIMES THREE
DIFFERENT COLOURED STRANDS
OF CREWELWOOL ARE BLENDED
TOGETHER IN THE NEEDLE
(*PHOTOGRAPH: EIRIAN SHORT*)

***Plate 70***
DAISY PURSE, 1991, DESIGNED
AND WORKED BY MAUREEN
KING USING TRADITIONAL
STUMPWORK TECHNIQUES IN
INNOVATIVE WAYS.
EXAMINE THIS CLOSELY AND
YOU WILL REALISE THAT THE
DESIGN FORMS A DAISY-CHAIN.
EACH PETAL IS EXQUISITELY
WORKED IN DETACHED
BUTTONHOLE STITCH. THE TINY
VIOLET AND PURPLE LILACS ARE
WORKED IN VERY SMALL
STRAIGHT STITCHES, FORMING
SEED STITCHES. THEIR COLOUR
COMPLEMENTS THE CENTRES OF
THE DAISIES WHICH ARE
COMPOSED OF MINUTE YELLOW
FRENCH KNOTS. NOTICE ALSO
HOW THE GREEN SILK OF THE
PURSE IS COMPLEMENTED BY THE
DELICATE RED TIPS OF SOME OF
THE DAISIES

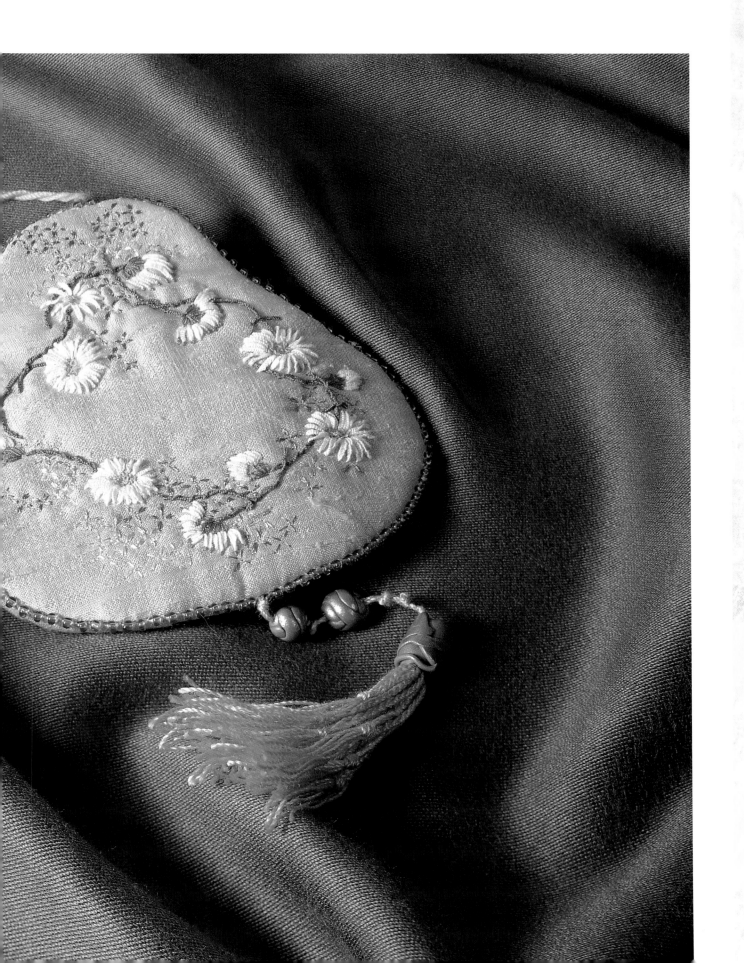

# *H*IGH SUMMER

## THE ROSE AND HERBACEOUS BORDERS

### THE ODOURS OF FLOWERS

*Thou perceivest the Flowers put forth their precious Odours,*
*And none can tell how from so small a centre comes such sweets,*
*First, e'er the morning breaks, joy opens in the flowery bosoms,*
*Joy even to tears, which the Sun rising dries; first the Wild Thyme*
*And Meadow-sweet, downy and soft waving among the reeds,*
*Light springing on the air, lead the sweet Dance: they wake*
*The Honeysuckle sleeping on the Oak; the flaunting beauty*
*Revels along upon the wind; the White-thorn, lovely May,*
*Opens her many lovely eyes listening; the Rose still sleeps,*
*None dare to wake her, soon she bursts her crimson curtain'd bed*
*And comes forth in the majesty of beauty; every Flower,*
*The Pink, the Jessamine, the Wall-flower, the Carnation,*
*The Jonquil, the mild Lilly, opes her heavens; every Tree*
*And Flower and Herb soon fill the air with an innumerable Dance,*
*Yet all in order sweet and lovely.*

WILLIAM BLAKE

Plate 71
'ALBERTINE ROSE'. OIL
PAINTING, 1990

We come now to late June, July and early August when roses grow in profusion and our flowerbeds are full of delphiniums, lupins, foxgloves, marigolds, cornflowers and large heavy-headed poppies. All is a riotous display of resplendent colour combinations, and the air is filled with delicious perfumes.

Within this chapter there are five projects: two for the rose, and three depicting certain flower combinations that can be found in our borders at this time. All five projects develop the methods and techniques which we have practised before, so that our knowledge is extended.

*Fig 12*
DIAGRAM ILLUSTRATING A
POSSIBLE ORDER AND
HIERARCHY OF THE ELEMENTS
WHICH CONTRIBUTE TO AN
HARMONIOUS COMPOSITION

# THE ROSE

*The Rose doth deserve the chief and prime place among all Floures what-so-ever: being not only esteemed for his beauty, vertues, and odiferous smell: but also because it is the honour and ornament of our English scepter ... which pleasant floures deserve the chief place in crownes and garlands.*

JOHN GERARD

FROM: *THE HERBAL OR GENERAL HISTORIE OF PLANTES*

According to Greek legend, the rose is the flower of love and it remains so to this day. It was created by Cloris, the goddess of flowers, who sought the help of Aphrodite, the goddess of love, who imbued it with beauty. The three Graces then endowed it with

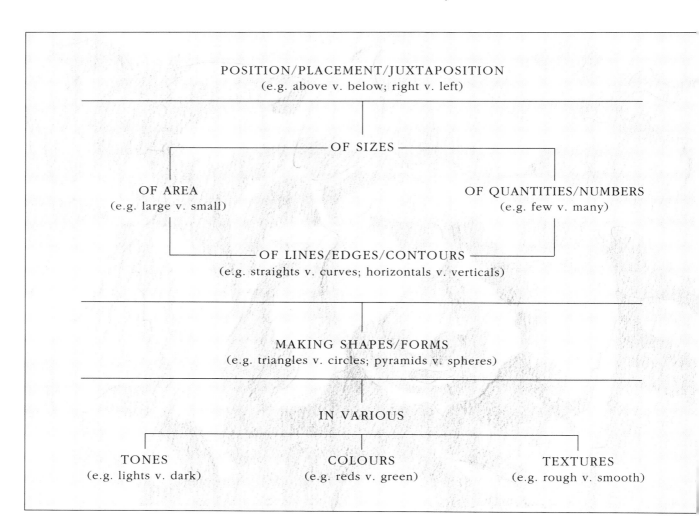

POSITION/PLACEMENT/JUXTAPOSITION
(e.g. above v. below; right v. left)

OF SIZES

OF AREA
(e.g. large v. small)

OF QUANTITIES/NUMBERS
(e.g. few v. many)

OF LINES/EDGES/CONTOURS
(e.g. straights v. curves; horizontals v. verticals)

MAKING SHAPES/FORMS
(e.g. triangles v. circles; pyramids v. spheres)

IN VARIOUS

TONES
(e.g. lights v. dark)

COLOURS
(e.g. reds v. green)

TEXTURES
(e.g. rough v. smooth)

charm, joy and brightness; and Dionysus, the god of wine, infused it with nectar so that it should emanate a sweet perfume. Finally Zephyr, the soft west wind, blew away the clouds so that Phoebus Apollo, the sun god, while riding his chariot through the sky, could shine his brilliant beams upon it and allow the flower to bloom. And so the rose became incarnate and was immediately pronounced the 'Queen of Flowers'.

### The First Rose Project

PLATE 71 is an illustration of a study I made in oils of the Albertine rose which flowers briefly, but nevertheless magnificently, for three weeks in June. This particular rose-tree was given to me as a 'thank-you' present by a delightful group of students after one of my 'Painting for the Petrified' courses. When I first planted the tree it was only two feet high; now it scrambles all over the south-facing wall of my home in Herefordshire.

In the three glorious weeks when the Albertine disperses its delicious favours, I anticipated a difficult decision: should I paint all of it, or just choose a small part? Remembering my own rules of procedure, I realised that all I had to do was to make a number of studies, each one dwelling on and emphasising a particular aspect or quality. Thus for our next project I chose just one full bloom, a few buds and several leaves; the rest is mainly wall.

In the early stages of our artistic and creative endeavours, many of us used to focus mainly on the 'subject' and deal with the 'background' later, as if it were an afterthought and not very important. Now, of course, we all realise that every part of a picture has its own importance, relative but equal. Mozart gave an interesting reply to the question 'What is the most important element in your music?': his answer was 'The silence', thus emphasising that the intervals and their particular durations between the notes are indeed crucial elements of the whole piece.

You will notice when you look at PLATE 72 that the methods and techniques which created the embroidery illustrated are those which we tried first with the plumbago project, and which we have practised several times since. However, when you engage in this and all subsequent projects hereafter, try to be even more aware of the important practice of balancing similar and contrasting elements in order to create the harmony in your composition. It is worthwhile pausing to elucidate this further.

*Art is harmony. Harmony is the analogy of contraries—the analogy of similarities of tone, of colour and of line.*

GEORGES SEURAT

It was this very statement by Georges Seurat, the post-Impressionist painter, which first pointed me in the positive and helpful direction of learning how to create a balanced harmony in my embroideries, paintings and drawings.

He mentions the three most important visual elements: tone, colour and line, which we use all the time, from our first cut into the fabric to the very last stitch. Let us examine each of these elements in turn and discover some examples of 'contraries' and 'similarities'.

*Tone* refers to the range of values between light and dark. Examples of contraries are contained in the way in which light blues contrast dark blues, and in which whites complement blacks. Examples of similarities are those very same four groups, namely the light blues, the dark blues, whites and blacks. You will remember in the first clematis project how we found slight variations in colours in our white and our black fabrics.

*Colour* refers to the differences between those qualities which we understand as red, orange, yellow and so forth. Look back to Figs 9 and 10 on p 66, and you will see the two diagrams of the colour wheel. The first diagram shows the complementary

*Plate 72* (OVERLEAF)
'ALBERTINE ROSE'. FABRIC
COLLAGE, MACHINE AND HAND
EMBROIDERY, 1992

pairs: red and green, blue and orange, yellow and violet; these are the contraries. Now look at the second diagram which has twelve sections: the colours which are next, or near to each other are known as 'analagous colours', for example blue-green, yellow-green and green-yellow. This is just one example of a similarity.

*Line* is a term which has a number of meanings. Here it is used specifically to refer to 'contour' or 'edge': there are straight edges or curved edges, and both groups are contrary, complementary and opposite to each other. All the straight lines are similar, as are all the curved lines.

The meeting of three straight lines and the closure of a curve form the two most fundamental shapes: the triangle and the circle. Wassily Kandinsky considered that these two forms were complementary, and he also said '... the impact of the acute angle on a triangle on a circle produces an effect no less powerful than the finger of God touching the finger of Adam in Michelangelo'.

There is another element which is very important to us embroiderers: *texture*, and of course texture is tactile rather than visual. Nevertheless I consider touching embroideries is just as important as looking at them. After all, we are continually touching them as we make them! Therefore we need to be aware of how we can repeat such things as hard shiny beads and contrast them with soft, matt fabric, or how we can use repeated raised areas with flat, smooth passages.

Perhaps even more crucial consideration needs to be given to those more subtle elements such as position, size and quantity which, in fact, govern and guide all the aforementioned actual elements. Remember, in our earlier projects, that I suggested percentages of how much thread and fabric should match or contrast each other in colour and tone. A close analogy can be made with a cooking recipe: there are not only the actual ingredients, but also the important aspects of measure, quantity, the order of mixing and the time of cooking. Fig 12 is a diagram with examples to help with such considerations, both for this and for future projects. As we continue with our first rose project, let us practise it together.

Use the fabric collage and machine embroidery methods in which you are now well practised. As you make every cut, every placement of fabric and every stitch, be looking all the time at Fig 12 and PLATE 72, and train your mind to follow this kind of thought process.

For the area of the wall, repeat similar hues of brown but contrast light browns with dark browns and blacks. This will also portray the illusion of shadows.

The hues of light brown are biased towards orange. Contrast these with very dark blue transparent material in the shadows, and very small vestiges of blue fabric as a component in the green leaves.

The areas of the wall are large. Contrast this size with small areas depicting the rose and the two buds.

The red colour of the rose and buds is analogous to the orange aspect of the wall, but being slightly more towards the violet category (crimson) it is distinct enough without protruding too much.

To represent the wall and the rose, cut both straight and curved edges in the fabric; but only cut curved edges for the petals; and very small, straight and thin-edged pieces for the stems.

Place curved edges in different directions and straight edges at different angles so both are complemented.

Place the small thin pieces which represent the stems in broken, curved lines and change their directions in a number of ways.

Contrast shiny and matt material and threads in all represented areas, but have more matt throughout so that the whole composition is not too brash.

Make looped stitches by hand and machine in all represented areas, but have more in the flowers and leaves so that they appear slightly more pronounced.

To prevent their protruding too much, make some loops in the same pale red in both the light parts of the rose and in the wall. This will also help to unify the composition.

Continue to think of ways to contrast and repeat the elements, which in combination will create the balanced harmony in your composition. Treat it rather like a guessing game, but do not worry if your 'answer' is right or wrong because until you try it, you will not know. Remember you can always redress an imbalance by adding or subtracting any of these elements—being creative is a state of continual flux, a never-ending process.

*Plate 73*
DETAIL OF A BERLINWORK AND
BEADWORK TEA COSY
FEATURING ROSES
(*HALL-TOWNLEY COLLECTION*)

*Plate 74*
EARLY TWENTIETH-CENTURY
PURSE, PROBABLY FRENCH,
EMBROIDERED WITH FINE
CANVASWORK ROSES
(*HALL-TOWNLEY COLLECTION*)

## The Second Rose Project

PLATE 75 illustrates a coloured pencil drawing of the yellow rose known as Canary Bird; it acts as the guide for this our next project.

Look now at PLATE 76 and you will see that we shall be practising the 'drawing with the needle' method with the sewing machine; this is the granite-stitch technique first used in the second daisy project (see p 103). However, this time the fabric is moved in much smaller and tighter circles in order to achieve a more subtle gradation of tones and colours.

Another development is that all six colours in the spectrum are used in the shadows. In the shadows of the yellow petals orange and violet (purple and magenta) were used in large quantities, with yellow, green, red and blue used in smaller amounts. The shadows around the roses were composed of various blues and greens in large quantities, with yellow, red, violet and orange used in smaller amounts. Thus here is another significant example of the importance of *measure* in our projects. Notice how all the same threads were used in both areas, but the effect is different because of a change in proportion.

(BELOW) *Plate 75*
'CANARY BIRD ROSE'.
COLOURED PENCIL DRAWING,
1991

(OPPOSITE) *Plate 76*
'CANARY BIRD ROSE'. MACHINE
EMBROIDERY, 1992

(OVERLEAF) *Plate 77*
'CORNFLOWERS AND
MARIGOLDS'. OIL PAINTING,
1978

Richard Box 1991

Richard Box Aug. '78

# THE THREE HERBACEOUS BORDER PROJECTS

Our first example is the vibrant juxtaposition of blue cornflowers with yellow and orange marigolds. The dazzling sight is achieved by the complementary pairing of orange and blue which enhance each other's company.

The oil painting illustrated in PLATE 77 is a study of such a scene, which I came upon quite unexpectedly. There I stayed for a whole week to paint four watercolours and two oil paintings. They have been an inspiration for many embroideries which I have made during a number of years.

PLATE 78 shows the most recent example. You will see that it has been made by the fabric collage and machine- and hand-embroidery method. Try following our well practised procedure, and if anything new or different occurs to you to try within the boundaries of the project, put it into practice immediately.

The new element in this work for me was at the very end when I decided to risk embroidering the entire surface with one of the Pfaff sewing machine's set patterns. I chose one that looked like a little star because it seemed to represent the gleams of light on these two flowers when they reflect the sunlight.

Our next two examples are the large-headed poppies with lupins; and delphiniums and lupins. I have linked the two projects together because not only did I make the two embroideries concurrently (PLATES 80 and 82) but also the two oil paintings which inspired them (PLATES 79 and 81). There were, in fact, four oil paintings painted in a week which resulted in a kind of joyful exhaustion! This some-

*Plate 78*
'CORNFLOWERS AND MARIGOLDS'. FABRIC COLLAGE, MACHINE AND HAND EMBROIDERY, 1992

*Plate 79*
'Poppies and Lupins'. Oil
painting, 1991

times happens when everything is flourishing at once and there is not a moment to lose.

In the making of both the paintings and the embroideries it was an extremely useful exercise to have more than one project going concurrently. As you know, I have urged you all through the book to put this way of working into practice. Just in case there are any readers who have not quite managed this yet, allow me to explain for the last time. If we get tired, it is good to have a rest, so why not engage in another project as you rest? The leaving of something often helps to solve difficult problems, and psychologically it is so comforting to have another alternative with which to take risks. This leads on to flexibility of mind and a transference of ideas. Indeed, it can liberate the creative spirit. Once more we have an example of how a rule can be the agent for freedom.

The method is as for the cornflower and marigold project, but these two have had much more time spent on them at the collage stage. I needed to cut the fabric pieces much smaller and more precisely than ever before. I believe I have influenced myself with my smaller 'drawing with the needle' projects in the kind of precision that can be achieved. However, I still wanted to portray the riot of sumptuous colour and texture which these two scenes deserve, as well as precision, and with this method the precision had to be done first rather than at the end because the richness of texture is created then with hand- and machine-made loops.

Enjoy your journey with these three projects, and maintain a carefree attitude; as J.F. Mill said, 'Genius can only breathe freely in an atmosphere of freedom!'.

*Plate 80* (OPPOSITE)
'POPPIES AND LUPINS'. FABRIC
COLLAGE, MACHINE AND HAND
EMBROIDERY, 1992

*Plate 81*
'DELPHINIUMS AND LUPINS'.
OIL PAINTING, 1991

*Plate 82* (OVERLEAF)
'DELPHINIUMS AND LUPINS'.
FABRIC COLLAGE, MACHINE AND
HAND EMBROIDERY, 1992

# *M* THE EADOW

The Poetry of earth is never dead:
When all the birds are faint with the hot sun
And hide in cooling trees, a voice will run
From hedge to hedge about the new-mown mead;
That is the Grasshopper's,--he takes the lead
In summer luxury,--he has never done
With his delights; for when tired out with fun
He rests at ease beneath some pleasant weed.
The poetry of earth is ceasing never:
On a lone winter evening, when the frost
Has wrought a silence, from the stove there shrills
The Cricket's song, in warmth increasing ever,
And seems to one in drowsiness half lost,
The Grasshopper's among some grassy hills.

JOHN KEATS

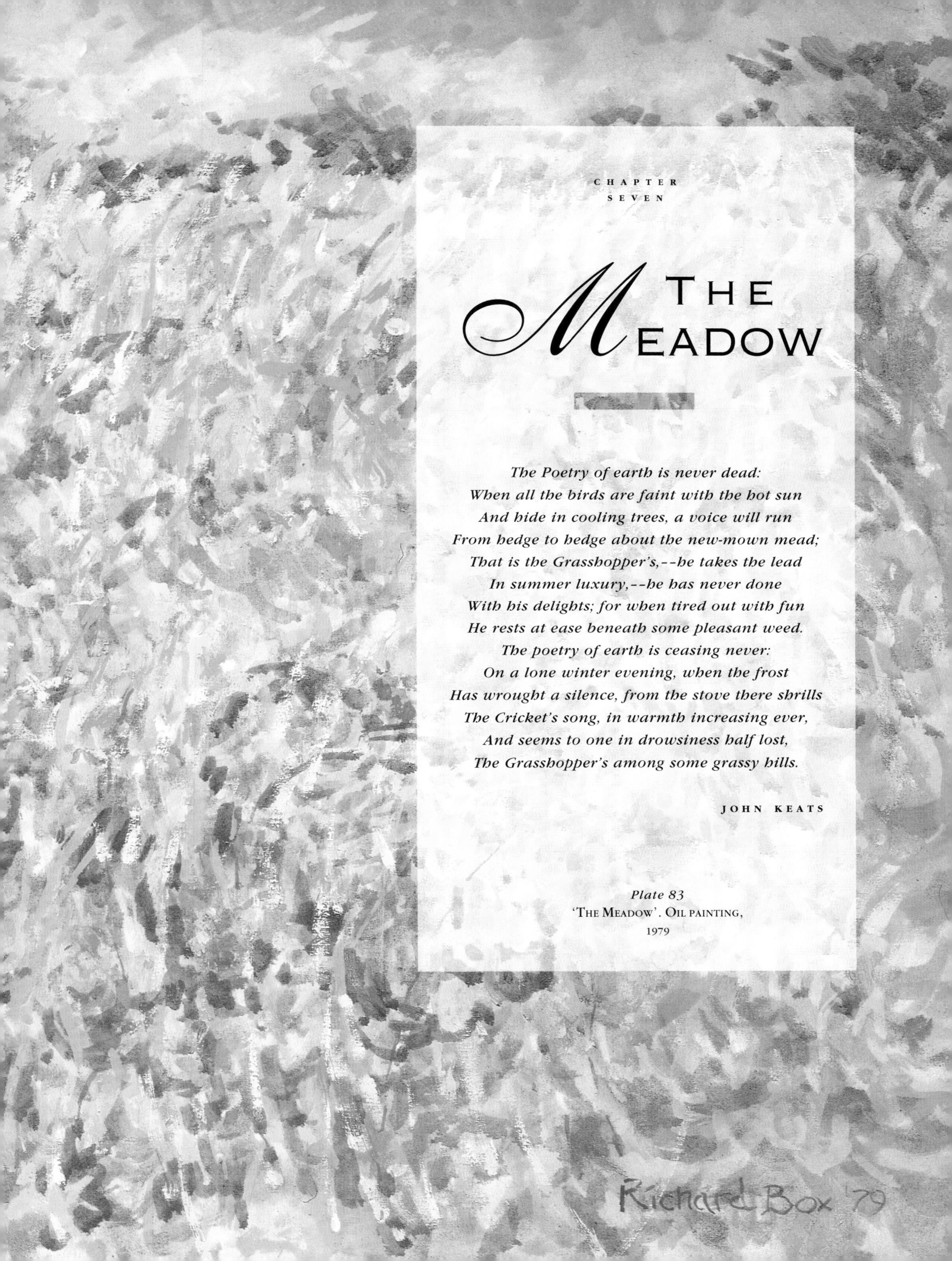

*Plate 83*
'THE MEADOW'. OIL PAINTING,
1979

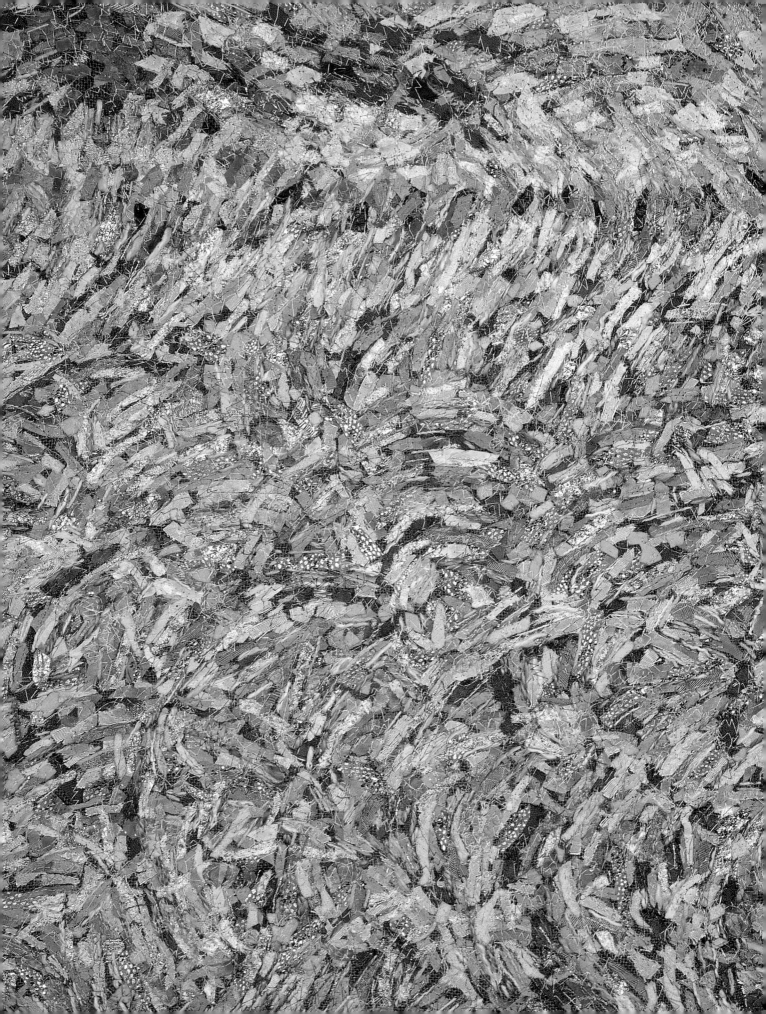

One sunny weekend in June, many years ago, I decided to take a walk along one of the Sussex footpaths; I skirted a number of fields banked by hedges filled with wild roses and finally came to a stile—I had to mount only the first step to glimpse a truly wonderful sight. There before me a meadow spread itself in all its glory. It was full of all kinds of wild flowers whose names were then beyond my knowledge, but whose colours captured my attention. It was as if they had made me their prisoner! The soft sound of the breeze gently rustling through the tops of the tall grasses, the grasshoppers chirruping amongst themselves, the buzz of the bees and the splash of colour of butterfly wings all augmented the splendour of the occasion. There was even a lark way up in the sky singing his heart out!

PLATE 83 illustrates a simple oil painting of this meadow, and I have chosen it to guide us through our last project.

Look now at PLATE 84, in which you will see I have used the fabric collage and machine and hand embroidery method. I cut the fabric pieces even smaller than I have ever done before, then laid them to form interlinking curved lines to represent the soft breezes wafting out of the sky, over the hedge and through the tall grasses and flowers of the meadow itself. Zigzag machine embroidery and straight hand-stitching emphasises this movement and completed the process. I was mindful of both van Gogh and Monet: van Gogh because of the energy he managed to impart to his landscapes, Monet because of the serenity of his last waterlily painting where there are no focal points. It is as if we are invited to enter and wander where we like at will.

I too invite you to enter and wander through my meadow at your leisure; and I hope you will enjoy making a meadow embroidery as the final project of this book, the one which will also be the first of all the projects that you do hereafter. And for each one of these, remember what Robert Bridges said: 'I too will something make and joy in the making'.

*Plate 84*
'THE MEADOW'. FABRIC
COLLAGE, MACHINE AND HAND
EMBROIDERY, 1992

# BIBLIOGRAPHY

ARNASON, H.H. *A History of Modern Art* Thames and Hudson, revised edition 1977

BENNINGFIELD, Gordon *Green and Pleasant Land* Viking, published by the Penguin Group 1989

BERRILL, Frances AND EXLEY, Helen *A Gift of Flowers* Exley Publishers Ltd 1983

BLOOMER, Carolyn M. *Principles of Visual Perception* van Nostrand, Reingold Company 1976

BONHAM-CARTER, Victor *A Posy of Wildflowers* Allan Wingate Ltd 1946

EDWARDS, Betty *Drawing on the Right Side of the Brain* Souvenir Press 1981

FRANK, Frederick *The Zen of Seeing* Vintage Books (originally published by Alfred A. Knopf) 1973

HAMILTON, George Heard *Painting and Sculpture in Europe 1880–1940* Penguin Books Ltd, revised edition; reprinted 1978

HANBURY, Ada *Flower Painting* Blackie and Son 1885

JEKYLL, Gertrude *Wood and Garden* The Ayer Company 1983

KERR, Jessica *Shakespeare's Flowers* Longman 1969

KLICKMAN, Flora *Flower Pictures by Maud Angell* London, 4 Bouverie St, early 1900s

KLICKMAN, Flora *Tramping with a Colour Box by C.J.Vine* London, 4 Bouverie St, early 1990s

LOWENFELD, **Victor** *Creative and Mental Growth* The Macmillan Company, fifth edition 1970

McKIM, **Robert H.** *Experiences in Visual Thinking* Wadsworth Incorporated, second edition 1980

MALINS, **Frederick** *Understanding Paintings: 'The Elements of Composition'* Phaidon Press Ltd 1980

MANTEGAZZA, **Paolo** *The Legends of Flowers* T.Werner Laurie Ltd 1930

MURRAY, **Peter and Linda** *A Dictionary of Art and Artists* Penguin Books Ltd, third edition; reprinted 1975

MUSSEN, **Paul H.**, LONGER, **John J.**, and KAGAN, **Jerome** *Child Development and Personality* Harper and Row, fifth edition 1979

**Not Ascribed** *Flower Lore* McCaw, Stevenson and Orr, before 1890

PICKLES, **Sheila** *The Language of Flowers* Pavilion Books Ltd 1990

RICHTER, **Irma A** *The Notebooks of Leonardo Da Vinci* Oxford University Press 1980

SEARLE, **Lindley (compiler)** *The Song of Flowers* Staples Press Ltd 1949

SHREE PUROHIT **Swami, and** YEATS, **W.B.(translator)** *The Ten Principal Upanishads* Faber and Faber Ltd 1970

SWAMI **Vivekananda** *Work and Its Secret* J.N. Dey at Union Press, seventh impression 1976

THOMAS, **Mary** *Dictionary of Embroidery Stitches* Hodder and Stoughton 1934

# GLOSSARY

Sometimes it is difficult to remember the meaning of certain words employed in an activity unfamiliar to you, even if the term is explained in the text. The following definitions indicate how certain words should be understood in this book.

ANALOGY Similarity, equivalent. For example: analogous colours are similar colours

APPLIQUÉ The application of one material to another by means of stitching

BALANCE Matching, bringing into equilibrium, regulating differences, equalisation

COLLAGE The application of one material to another by means of sticking with an adhesive

COLOUR The constituent parts of decomposed rays of light, and the general name given to those elements such as red, orange, yellow, green, blue and violet

COMPLEMENTARY Refers to an element or quality which usually contrasts with, or is in opposition to, another element or quality

COMPOSITION The harmonious relation of all parts, elements and qualities of a whole

CONCURRENT The undertaking, or existing together of two or more activities to which attention is given alternately but not simultaneously

CONTRAST The emphasis of differences between things, elements or qualities by close juxtaposition

COUCHING A form of stitching where one or more threads are attached to material by another thread

CROSS-HATCHING A method of drawing by means of crossed parallel lines in order to achieve a type of shading or certain coloured effects

DESIGN The plan or organisation of all parts of an activity or embroidery or any created object to compose a coherent order and unity

HARMONY The balanced combination of constituent

parts, elements and qualities to form a connected whole, which are usually similar and complementary

HUE The quality that distinguishes one particular kind of colour from another, such as a blue-green and a yellow-green

INTEGRITY The state of wholeness and completeness; entire, in and of itself

LINE An edge or contour in either a straight or a curved direction

LOCAL COLOUR The intrinsic colour of any particular object such as a *yellow* buttercup

LOCAL COLOUR TONE The intrinsic tonal value of any particular object, such as a *pale*-blue plumbago

PERCEPTION The detection, recognition and understanding of sensations received from stimuli within the environment

PROCEDURE The particular way of conducting, organising and moving through a process or activity

PROCESS An activity or course of actions

SEED STITCH A very small, straight stitch which can be made at any angle

SHADE A dark tone

SHAPE An area perceived in two dimensions

SPATIAL Refers to the ability to understand how individual parts relate to each other

STRAIGHT STITCHING By hand: single stitches of any desired length or angle; by machine: continuous line consisting of single stitches, in any direction

STUMP-WORK Embroidery stitches and devices which are raised in relief from a ground fabric

TENT STITCH A diagonal canvas-work stitch

TEXTURE The surface quality of any physical substance

TINT A light or pale tone

TONE The quality that refers to any value which is within the range between light and dark

# ACKNOWLEDGEMENTS

I am indebted to many organisations and individuals for their part in the production of this book. I now take this happy opportunity to give them my thanks for all their encouragement and help.

To Jean Ainsworth, Annya Barber, Sally and Sue Blenkinsop, Ann Clark, Jane Close, The Embroiderers' Guild, Pauline Farrar, Greta and Mike Fitchett, Margaret Hall-Townley, Jill Irving, Anne Jones, Maureen and Tony King, Audrey Loxton, Suzie MacDonald, Juliet Pollard, Jo Pickering, Eirian Short, Phyllis Smith, Sonja Turner of Special Courses, Lichfield, and all those who asked to remain anonymous for being kind enough to lend my work from their collections.

To Vivienne Wells, my editor, for her useful guidance and kind assurances. To Dudley Moss for his beautiful photography throughout the book. To Pauline Garnham for her time and patience in typing the manuscript.

Finally, to all those students who have enjoyed my courses, and who continually encourage me in my teaching.

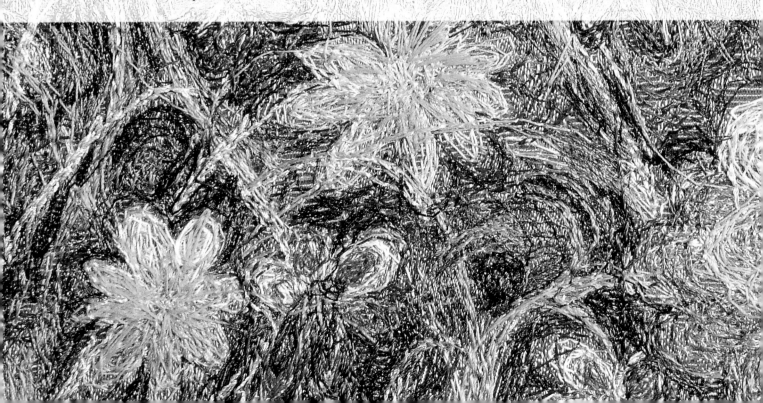

# INDEX

Entries in *italic* indicate illustrations.